ALASKA

Valdez

BLIGH ISLAND

Port Fidalgo

NAKED ISLAND

Port Gravina

PRINCE WILLIAM
SOUND

Orca Bay

Cordova

HAWKINS ISLAND

CHENEGA ISLAND

KNIGHT ISLAND

HINCHINBROOK ISLAND

GREEN ISLAND

MONTAGUE ISLAND

YAKUTAT BAY

Yakutat

Situk River

Ahrnklin River

Dangerous River

GULF OF ALASKA

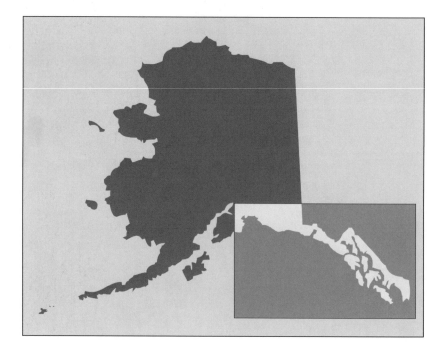

PACIFIC OCEAN

BEAR MAN
OF ADMIRALTY ISLAND

Allen Hasselborg at Hasselborg Lake, Admiralty Island, 1925.
Photograph by C. Day. Courtesy of E. Gardner

BEAR MAN
OF ADMIRALTY ISLAND

A BIOGRAPHY OF
ALLEN E. HASSELBORG

JOHN R. HOWE

 University of Alaska Press
LanternLight Library
Fairbanks, Alaska

Library of Congress Cataloging-in-Publication Data

Howe, John R.
    Bear man of Admiralty Island : a biography of Allen E. Hasselborg
    / John R. Howe.
        p.   cm.
    Includes bibliographical references and index.
    ISBN 0-912006-80-3 (cloth : alk. paper). -- ISBN
    0-912006-81-1 (pbk. : alk. paper)
    1. Hasselborg, Allen E., 1876-1956. 2. Naturalists--Alaska-
    -Biography. 3. Alaska--Biography. 4. Brown bear--Alaska.
    I. Title.
    QH31.H355H68   1996
    508'.092--dc20   96-12930
    [B]   CIP

University of Alaska Press
        First Printing, 1996
        Second Printing, 1999
International Standard Book Number: cloth 0-912006-80-3
                                     paper 0-912006-81-1
Library of Congress Catalog Number: 96-12930
Printed in the United States of America by Thomson-Shore, Inc.
This publication was printed on acid-free paper that meets the minimum
requirements for the American National Standard for Information Science—Perma-
nence of Paper for Printed Library Materials ANSIZ39.48-1984.

Publication coordination and production by Pamela Odom.
Cover and text design by Paula Elmes.
Text typeface Adobe Apollo®Display typeface Adobe Castellar®
Cover photograph of entrance to Seymour Canal, 1984, by John Howe.
Back cover photograph of Allen Hasselborg, 1925, by Charles Day.

To my parents, Calderon and Sarah A. Howe, and their respect for the English language.

CONTENTS

ACKNOWLEDGMENTS

IN 1949, *TRUE* MAGAZINE published a story about Hasselborg being mauled by a bear. When a Juneau newspaper reporter asked him what he thought of it, Hasselborg said that many of its facts were wrong. "They tell me they have to dress bear stories up to make them interesting," he added, "as if the truth isn't interesting enough!"*

I kept that statement taped to my computer during much of the time I was researching and writing this book, both to remind myself of an essential aspect of Hasselborg's character, and to keep myself honest as I tried to tell the story of a recluse who died more than thirty years ago, didn't talk much, and wrote letters only as an infrequent, painful chore. I never met him. I wish I had. I hope that my attempts to express my understanding of who he was and what motivated him are both sufficiently documented and modest enough that I haven't overstepped the bounds of poetic license or legitimate psychological theory. While many people helped me get to know Hasselborg, I alone am responsible for my conclusions about him in this book. My descriptions of southeastern Alaska come from the twelve years I lived in Juneau and the total of about five months I spent on

---

* "Allen Hasselborg Says Bear Stories Don't Need Dressing," *Daily Alaska Empire,* 2 October 1950.

Admiralty Island during that period exploring, hunting, and working as a production assistant for a film about Alaska coastal brown bears. The reader should also be aware that all quotations from Hasselborg's letters and other personal documents have been transcribed exactly as he wrote them and thus include his misspellings and incorrect punctuation.

Most of my information about Hasselborg's childhood came from "Not for All the Laurel Grows," the unpublished memoirs of his sister, Flora Hasselborg Merritt. I was very fortunate that Mrs. Merritt had such a keen memory, a sharp eye for human behavior, a fine wit, and the skill to tell her family's story so well. Several dozen letters Hasselborg wrote to his family between 1899 and 1955 form the backbone of my account of his adult life. For the use of that material, and for her hospitality and wise insights into the Hasselborg family, I am very grateful to Mrs. Merritt's daughter, Elinor Gardner.

I thank Mrs. Gardner for the use of Hasselborg's copies of two books by John M. Holzworth, *The Wild Grizzlies of Alaska*, and *The Twin Grizzlies of Admiralty Island*. Hasselborg's many notes in the margins were crucial to my understanding of an important period of his life. *Hunting American Bears*, by Frank C. Hibben, also has several chapters based on Hibben's experiences hunting and photographing bears with Hasselborg. Raymond Sheppard, Jr., Hasselborg's great-nephew, kindly loaned me the copy his Uncle Allen had marked up and corrected. Those annotations, along with several dozen letters from Hasselborg to Raymond Sheppard, were very helpful. Thanks also to Mrs. Sheppard and Linda Sheppard for their hospitality and for the use of a number of Sheppard family letters and photographs.

A number of other people took an interest in this book, providing me with everything from food and lodging, to photographs and other crucial information, computer time, advice, and just plain encouragement: Arne Albrecht (U.S. Forest Service); Greg Blair and Robert D. Fisher (National Museum of Natural History); Archie Brodsky and Bill Boggs (National Writers Union); Jeff Brown and Judy Alaback (KTOO-FM, Juneau); Victor H. Cahalane; Gene Christman, Barbara Stein, Karen Klitz (University of California Museum of Vertebrate Zoology); Harold J. Coolidge; Trevor Davis; Bob De Armond; Frederica de Laguna (Bryn Mawr College); William P. Gee (U.S. Forest Service); E. Raymond Hall (University of Kansas); Frank and Eleanor Hibben; Rob Gardner; Ron Klein (Northlight); Karl Lane; Jeff Leer (University of Alaska); Don McKnight (Alaska Department of Fish and Game); John Merritt; K. J. Metcalf and Madonna Moss (Admiralty Island National Monument); John Neary (U.S. Forest Service); Mary R. Patton (Oregon Historical Society); Verda Carey, Gladi Kulp, and Phyliss De Muth (Alaska Historical Library); Stan Price; Ron Smith; Lewis Schnaper; Bob and Elaine Schroeder; Mark Wittow; Helen and Bruce White (Minnesota Historical Society); and Ralph Young.

I also thank Debbie (Van Stone) Gonzalez of the University of Alaska Press, who encouraged me to revise a skinny, earlier version. Her colleague, Pam Odom, patiently and ably managed the complex task of turning the manuscript into a book.

I am especially grateful to the Alaska Historical Commission for funding my early research outside Alaska, and to Linda Daniel for her crucial, last minute research assistance; to Bruce Howe, Brad Matsen, and Dick Nelson, who reviewed a first draft; to the Juneau Arts and Humanities Council for financial support down the home stretch; to Linda Daniel, Dave Hunsaker, and Roger Pasquier for editing and proofing a near-final draft; to Joel Bennett and Luisa Stoughton, co-founders of the Allen Hasselborg Fan Club, who handed me many tickets for this journey; and to my wife, Anne-Marie, for all her patient support, and for teaching me to begin to hear the ancient language of the bear.

CHRONOLOGY

1908:   Member of 1908 Alexander Alaska Expedition, Prince William Sound.

1909:   Finishes building the *Ebba*, his first launch; collects specimens in southeast Alaska for University of California Museum of Vertebrate Zoology.

1911:   Begins hunting bears for Dr. C. H. Merriam.

1912:   Mauled by bear at Glacier Bay.

1913–1917:   Lives on Douglas Island, building dories for sale.

1916:   Finishes building new launch, the *Bulldogg*.

1917:   Settles at Mole Harbor, Admiralty Island.

1925:   Guides Harold J. Coolidge and Charles Day on bear hunt.

1926:   Receives patent to Mole Harbor homestead; first visit from John Holzworth; "Save-the-Bear Campaign" begins.

1935:   Buys last guiding license.

1938/1939:   Mauled by bear at Pleasant Bay, Admiralty Island.

1953:   Sells Mole Harbor homestead.

1954:   Leaves for Washington, D.C., and Florida.

1955:   Returns to Alaska, admitted to Sitka Pioneers' Home.

1956:   Dies February 19 in Sitka hospital.

INTRODUCTION

ON JULY 12, 1893, at the World's Columbian Exposition in Chicago, a young professor named Frederick Jackson Turner presented a paper that would make a lasting impression on scholarly thinking about the significance of the frontier in American history. Pointing to figures in the 1890 U.S. census that showed an average of two or more people per square mile throughout the West, Turner announced that vast uninhabited public lands were no longer available to nurture independence and self-reliance in the American character.[1]

To the student of Alaska history it is not surprising that in his landmark paper Turner failed to mention a frontier almost a third as large as all the western states and territories combined. Because of its cold climate and great distance from the rest of the nation, Alaska had been largely ignored by most Americans during the quarter century that had passed since the United States bought it from Russia. Its population of 35,000 had not grown at all. In 1893, the year Turner made his startling announcement, it still had no organized government, no delegate to Congress, no criminal code, and no land laws that encouraged settlement.

Three years later, gold was discovered in the Yukon Territory, and as thousands of fortune-seekers poured through Alaska on their way to the gold fields, Americans and much of the world became aware for the first time of a vast new territory to the north. By the turn of the century, Alaska's population had almost doubled, and the image of a new frontier hero had emerged in the nation's consciousness: the Alaska sourdough, a winterized version of a California Forty-Niner surrounded by sled dogs, Eskimos, hungry wolves, and not much else besides ice and snow.

The Klondike fever soon abated, however, and The Great Land slipped back into obscurity. Neglected by politicians in Washington, D.C., who insisted on seeing it as a distant and mostly worthless icebox inhabited by Natives and foolhardy white adventurers, it would struggle until 1959, longer than any territory in American history, to win the rights and privileges of statehood.

For the purposes of this biography, it is a nice coincidence that only two months after Turner read his famous paper in Chicago, Allen Hasselborg happened to be in that city buying rifle ammunition at Montgomery Wards. He was seventeen years old at the time, traveling with his family to their new homestead in Florida. Six years later he left home again, this time on his own, headed north and west. He first saw Alaska from the deck of a fishing schooner in 1899, three years after the Klondike strike. By 1901 he was living in the southeastern panhandle, and he would not set foot outside Alaska again until 1954, two years before he died.

In many ways he was similar to the pioneers extolled by Turner: independent of mind, tough as nails, suspicious of government, and possessing a wide range of skills required for survival in a wild, often harsh new land. During different periods of his life Hasselborg was a miner, prospector, bear hunter, boat builder, trapper, fisherman, hunting guide, and homesteader. Alone he cleared more than ten acres of old-growth forest in Bunyanesque style. He trapped beaver with all the skill of a Colorado mountain man, guided natural history expeditions reminiscent of Lewis and Clark's, had hostile encounters with Indians and more than his share of run-ins with bears.

Yet the frontier he knew was far removed in time from Turner's frontier. It would be closed not by barbed wire, telegraph lines, and railroads but by airplanes, radios, and the Second World War. And southeastern Alaska is a world apart from the American West—even from the tundra and birch forests of interior Alaska popularized during the Klondike rush. A maze of mountainous islands cast up against a mountainous coast, it is a land of soft rain and drifting mists; lush forests of towering spruce and hemlock; glaciers thundering ice into the sea; dark, stormy winters with howling north winds; and moist, gentle summers when the days last almost until midnight, and spawning salmon swim thick in the streams, a feast for bald eagles, ravens, and Alaska coastal brown bears, the largest carnivorous land mammals on earth.

It is with those huge relatives of the grizzly bear that Hasselborg's name is now most closely associated. In many ways, throughout his life, his fascination with them determined what he did, where he went, and whom he knew. The market for Alaska bear pelts at the turn of the century gave him his first real opportunity to earn a living at something he liked doing and did well. In 1907, Anne M. Alexander, an amateur naturalist interested in bears, hired him as a guide and hunter for a scientific expedition to southeastern Alaska. By the end of that summer she had given his name to a lake and a river on Admiralty Island, a wilderness near Juneau with a large population of brown bears.

Miss Alexander hired him again to collect bear specimens and guide her expedition to Prince William Sound the following year, which further broadened his scientific knowledge and

Prince William Sound, 1908 Alexander Alaska Expedition. *Courtesy of University of California Museum of Vertebrate Zoology*

cemented several professional relationships that would provide a substantial portion of his income for the next decade. In 1912, while collecting for C. H. Merriam, an influential former director of the U.S. Biological Survey, he was mauled by a brown bear, barely escaping with his life. That made him decide to build a house near Juneau and try to earn a living as a boat builder. But Dr. Merriam's demand for bear specimens soon lured him back to Admiralty Island. He filed for a homestead there in 1917 and lived alone among the bears for the next thirty-seven years.

Though he continued to guide hunters for many years after he settled at Mole Harbor, he wouldn't let anyone shoot bears near his homestead. In the early 1930s, several photographers and conservationists he had taken to photograph wildlife led a national campaign to protect Admiralty Island from a proposed logging project. As a year-round resident of the island and an acknowledged expert on bears, Hasselborg was drawn deep into the fray. Two books and several magazine articles were written about him, and he was quoted in newspaper articles and in testimony before congressional committees. Though the Save-the-Bear controversy gave him a small measure of fame, it made him decide to quit guiding and live in seclusion for most of the rest of his life.

Yet Hasselborg's knowledge of bears went far deeper than the understanding of an experienced sportsman or naturalist. He was possessed by them, from his childhood, when he had a pet raccoon (a distant cousin of the bear), to just before he died, when he dreamt that bears were coming to take him away. On more than one occasion people heard him talking to bears and the bears responding as if they understood what he was saying. One hunter saw him strip blueberries off bushes and swallow them along with their leaves and stems. "If you're ever going to become a bear hunter," Hasselborg explained, "you've got to eat like a bear and live like a bear, then maybe someday you'll start to think like a bear."[2]

Many cultures tell stories about bears becoming people and people becoming bears, perhaps because bears resemble us so much, both behaviorally and physically. As Paul Shepard and Barry Sanders explain in *The Sacred Paw,*

> Like us, the bear stands upright on the soles of his feet, his eyes nearly in a frontal plane. The bear moves his forelimbs freely in their shoulder sockets, sits on his tail end, one leg folded, like an

adolescent slouched at a table, worries with moans and sighs, courts with demonstrable affection, produces excrement similar to man's, snores in his sleep, spanks his children, is avid for sweets, and has a moody, gruff, and morose side. The bear is himself a creature in his own right, needing no justifying or compliance with human purpose. Try as we may, however, the bear's independence is hard for us to allow, for we cannot shake off the impression that behind the long muzzle and beneath the furry coat so unlike our naked skin there is a self not so different from us. . . .[3]

It is the bear's broad, searching, persistent openness that makes contact with us, that flash of recognition in which men instantly perceive a fellow being whose questing provocation, whose garrulous, taciturn, lazy ways, even whose obligations and commitments to hunt, to hole up, and to dominate the space he lives in are familiar.[4]

Because they disappear into the earth during the winter and reemerge in the spring, because they forage for a wide variety of plants and animals available only at certain times of the year, bears have also long been honored for their knowledge of the seasons, the cosmic cycle of death and rebirth.

The Tlingits, the Alaska Natives with whom Hasselborg had the most contact during his lifetime, held the brown bear in particularly high regard. Bear skins lined the beds of Tlingit children to ward off illness, and bear bones, claws, paws, and teeth were worn as ornaments and amulets.[5] Strict rules and rituals governed Tlingit relations with bears, as they believed that bears could understand human speech and read human thoughts. Tlingit

Brown bears, Admiralty Island, 1931. From film, *The Great Bear of Alaska*,
by William Finley and Arthur Pack of the American Nature Association.
Courtesy of the Oregon Historical Society

hunters were particularly careful to handle the head of a slain
bear properly. After carrying it back to camp, they decorated it
with eagle feathers and set it by a fire to keep it warm, thus
assuring the bear's spirit they meant no disrespect.[6]

Certainly during most of Hasselborg's thirty-six-year career
as a hunter and guide, bear skins and skulls were no more to him
than rewards from successful hunts. Yet he apparently gave
some credence to the Tlingit belief that bears were offended if
humans spoke disrespectfully to them.[7] Living alone among bears
for so many years on Admiralty Island, watching them through

Allen Hasselborg's cabin at Mole Harbor, 1930s or early 1940s, long view.
Courtesy of F. Hibben

so many seasons, surely he came to know some of their cosmic power.

That simple, self-reliant, day-to-day existence alone in the wilds of Admiralty Island was the essence of his life. He was determined to live that way. When he was almost seventy years old, his friend from the Alexander Expeditions, Joe Dixon, wrote to say that Miss Alexander herself much admired his independence. "She said a lot of nice things about you being about the finest woodsman she had ever met," Dixon said, "but I think the thing she admired most is that you have lived your life in your own way, the way you wanted it, without being dependent on others."[8] He knew it was a life worth living, one that others might envy. In a letter to his sister Flora, he reported that the grandson of Ralph Waldo Emerson and two other eminent Bostonians had come to Mole Harbor: "Who was it wrote about the fellow that made the mousetrap and they wore a beaten path to his door?" he asked. "Seems to me it was old Emerson. Well grandson Raymond Emerson and his wife among others came up the muddy trail to my shack and he slept on the floor for a few nights."[9]

So it wasn't just wilderness and brown bears that drew visitors to Mole Harbor. Allen Hasselborg was an intriguing, often startling man, charismatic enough to attract much attention during his lifetime. Everyone I asked about him had admired or at least respected him. Some remembered him as an intimidating, eccentric old hermit; others recalled that he was fascinating company and a loyal friend. One woman described him as "a fine man," "a scamp," and "a queer duck" all in the same breath.[10] And almost without fail their reminiscences brought up nostalgia for the years before the Second World War, when some of the territory still hadn't been mapped, when you knew almost everyone you passed on the street in Juneau, when you relied less on the government and more on yourself and your neighbors—"back before there was any law,"[11] as Hasselborg himself once put it, when Alaska was truly The Last Frontier.

"They tell me they have to dress bear stories up to make them interesting, as if the truth isn't interesting enough."

—Allen Hasselborg, 1950

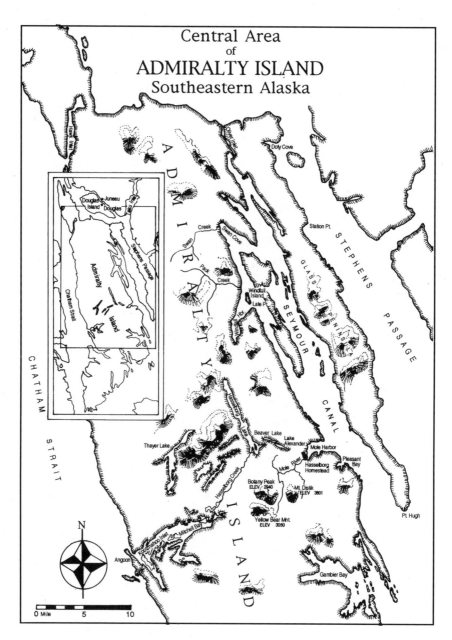

Central Area of Admiralty Island (southeastern Alaska).
Map by Elizabeth C. Franky

1

HASSELBORG'S

DOMAIN

ALLEN HASSELBORG came into Juneau only a few times a year. To visit him, you had to go by boat seventy miles south to his homestead at Mole Harbor, a secluded bay near the middle of Admiralty Island. Even when you were safely past the reefs at the mouth of Mole Harbor, if the tide was low, a mile of mud flats still lay between you and his cabin. So you anchored up and cut the engine, and the island came out to greet you with the soft, liquid call of a thrush, the salty stench of seaweed, the dark green forest looming behind the beach.

As you rowed in to shore, you would become aware of Hasselborg standing quietly waiting for you at the edge of the water, a rifle cradled in one arm. The rifle made you a little nervous, especially if you hadn't met him before. Though he owned about a hundred acres at the head of the bay, everyone in town knew that all of Mole Harbor was Hasselborg's domain. Back in the 1920s the U.S. Forest Service had tried to evict him, and he responded by firing across the bow of a service boat as soon as it entered the bay. More than twenty years had passed since then,

Allen Hasselborg at Mole Harbor, 1931.
Courtesy of Oregon Historical Society

and Hasselborg was well into his sixties, but he still wasn't someone you wanted to bother. "We showed Allen Hasselborg great deference," a friend once said. "Everyone did, of course. His was a personality that demanded respect."[1]

Though of medium height, he had the broad shoulders of a woodsman and thick legs of a mountaineer—a good-looking man (women remembered that) with a full beard, ruddy cheeks, a slightly aquiline nose, and hazel-green eyes that pierced right through you. "His face was kindly, but with a peculiar alertness, a certain air of questioning as though he were awaiting our next move, or perhaps watching for a mistake," one visitor recalled.[2] Usually he'd be wearing an old round-brimmed canvas hat, a frayed cotton shirt patched at the elbows, and baggy wool pants tucked into black rubber boots.

If you had come on any kind of government business, you knew you were in for a hard time; you did your business right there on the beach and were glad to finish it and leave. If you told him you were a scientist, your knowledge would immediately be put to the test. If you were out hunting, you were sternly informed that no hunting was allowed at Mole Harbor. More often than not, if you passed inspection—especially if he knew you—Hasselborg invited you back to his cabin.

So you followed behind him along the beach to the mouth of Mole River, feeling a bit loud and clumsy behind his quiet, graceful stride. All the while you kept a sharp eye out for his bears. Everyone thought of them that way—as his; he had names for most of them and wouldn't let anyone hunt them. Especially during the summer, when salmon were spawning in the river, they were around all the time. No matter how many brown bears you'd seen before, it was always unnerving when one came ambling along the riverbank or plowing toward you through the tall grass in Hasselborg's meadow, with the flowing grace of a cat. You didn't want to think about trying to outrun them, and when they raised up on their hind legs to look around, it was all too easy to see how big they were. Some of the males at Hasselborg's place stood well over eight feet tall and must have weighed about a thousand pounds. It didn't help much when he dismissed your concern with a wave of his hand. "That's Dark Pants," he told one anxious visitor, "he lives here."[3] To him, the bears at Mole Harbor were big, unruly pets—interesting and entertaining, but mostly just a nuisance when they dug up his potatoes or trampled the other vegetables in his garden.

His cabin first came into view around the first bend in the river. Visitors were always struck by how tiny it looked with Mt. Distik, a thirty-eight-hundred-foot peak, rising right behind it. Twenty by twenty-five feet, it was one room with a lean-to shed.[4] You went in through the shed, a workshop cluttered with boots, pack frames, axes, traps, outboard engines, and all the other well-worn tools and equipment of a self-sufficient homesteader. Hasselborg would show you in with what one visitor described as "the grave courtesy of a king ushering a subject into his castle."[5]

Inside, everything was neat and clean. "Often men who live alone are prone to sloppy habits, but not Allen," recalled Amos Burg, a photographer from Juneau. "He was fastidious. His clothes were neatly patched, washed and clean. Every few days he trimmed his whiskers. He scrubbed his dishes in hot water."[6] Each corner of the cabin had a specific function, as if it were a separate room in a much larger house. Visitors were always required to follow a strict protocol. "One simply was not allowed to eat [one's] stew in the living room," one woman remembered.[7] What Hasselborg called the "living room" or "sitting room" was an old easy-chair in front of the only window, which looked out on Mole River. The "kitchen" was to the right of the door as you came in: a cupboard, a table with two chairs, and a wood stove with pots and pans hanging on the wall behind it. To the left of the door were more shelves and a small table that was the "washroom" or "gun room," where he kept soap, a wash basin, a towel, medicine, chemicals, firearms, and ammunition. The "library"—shelves stocked with dozens of books—was just past the sitting room. Along the back wall, a narrow stairway led up to his sleeping loft. Ralph Young, a bear hunting guide, once sneaked a look at the loft and saw an enormous bear rug on the floor, one of the biggest he had ever seen.[8]

If a visitor could stay for a while, Hasselborg made tea, and before long there would be some good conversation, though it always took the host a while to get going. "He wasn't real talkative, but he would answer you, even talk at length when you asked him things," said Stan Price, who knew Hasselborg in his later years.[9] "He was courteous but stern and distant, well-spoken but not talkative," another acquaintance recalled.[10] He spoke quietly and precisely, occasionally gesturing with his hands, rarely laughing or smiling, though when he did, it was enough to crinkle the skin at the corners of his eyes.

"He talked about everything from the origin of the Latter Day Saints and the relation of the Essenes to pre-evangelical Christianity to the present day sea weed industry in Japan and political conditions in modern Europe," a college professor wrote soon after meeting Hasselborg for the first time.[11] "His information was not pedantic or strained; it was as modest as it was accurate. He has an unusually retentive memory and possesses the rare ability to use the knowledge which he has accumulated through years of reading. . . . He seldom makes general statements without specific examples to back them up."[12] "It was a joy to talk to this self-educated man on almost any subject, because he had been an extensive reader," another visitor, a Harvard student, recalled. "His knowledge of Shakespeare was phenomenal."[13]

Interior of Allen Hasselborg's cabin at Mole Harbor,
c. 1930. *Courtesy of Sheppard family*

Dean Goodwin, a pilot who for many years flew mail to a cannery near Mole Harbor, often wondered how much Hasselborg's books weighed.

> He had literally hundreds of pounds of literature on botany and geology. He was well-educated, very well-educated. It made you wonder. I remember one time talking to him and something came up about water flow and he got out this old chunk of pencil and a piece of paper and did mathematics in a few minutes that it would take me half an hour to do with an adding machine.[14]

If the conversation warmed up, Hasselborg would get out his tin box of old photographs taken back when he was hunting bears for the Smithsonian and guiding scientists and wildlife photographers. He liked talking about bears and politics but not about his family or why he came to Alaska. To some extent, that was typical of an Alaskan: when you came the great distance up to the country, by choice or necessity, you left some of your past behind. Yet Hasselborg was so mysterious, and so impressive somehow that for a while he was rumored to be the son of a Scottish lord who led the first pioneers into Minnesota. "There is a tradition in Alaska that I am the lost son and heir of the Earl of Selkirk," Hasselborg remarked in 1930, "and am expected to allways deny it!!?"[15]

2

MINNESOTA

UPBRINGING

THE EARLIEST EVIDENCE of Allen Hasselborg's presence in the world comes from a story told by one of his sisters.[1] According to Flora Hasselborg, soon after Allen was born, their mother got fed up with their father's habit of loaning money to the neighbors and decided to collect some of the debts herself. One of the debtors, a photographer, pleaded poverty, so she made him take a picture of her holding baby Allen on her lap. Many years later, Flora would recall that in that tintype portrait (now long since lost) Mary Hasselborg looked "mad enough to eat nails."

Given how that baby turned out, it's tempting to imagine that his expression was at least as indignant as his mother's. Suffice it to say that Mary Ballard Hasselborg knew the value of a dollar and wasn't a woman to be trifled with. She liked to say that her ancestors came to America in 1635, only a few years after the *Mayflower*, and that she was descended from Israel Putnam, a Revolutionary War hero. Some Mohawk Indian blood

Mary Ballard Hasselborg, Allen
Hasselborg's mother, c. 1870.
Courtesy of E. Gardner

was added to the family line by her great-great-grandmother. Her great-grandfather, Jeremiah Ballard, was a Vermont preacher blacklisted by his fellow Methodists for displaying what one contemporary historian described as arrogance and impenitence. Maybe as a result of that religious altercation, Jeremiah's son landed in Illinois, where Mary's father, Charles, was born. Charles married a Scottish girl from Kentucky who died soon after giving birth to Mary, their fifth child.

Within a few years, Charles Ballard had married a widow with six children and a nasty disposition. By the time Mary was eight, the Civil War had begun and all of her brothers and sisters had left home. For the next seven years she was alone and miserable with her stepmother, who often beat her. At the age of fifteen,

Olaf Hasselborg, Allen Hasselborg's father. "He had black hair, a fine high forehead, ice blue eyes, a Roman nose, and I never knew what his mouth and chin were like because he always wore a beard." *Flora Hasselborg Merritt, "Not for All the Laurel Grows." Courtesy of E. Gardner*

11

she ran away. She was taken in by a Ballard uncle, but soon left to work in several factories before finding a teaching job in Franconia, Minnesota. There she met Olaf Hasselborg, a handsome, forty-nine-year-old bachelor living alone in a big house. He was well-educated and a skilled cabinetmaker. After so much unhappiness, first cooped up with a mean stepmother, then on the road, bouncing from job to job, Mary was more than ready to settle down. Though he was twenty-six years older and she barely knew him, when Mr. Hasselborg proposed, she readily accepted. They were married a year later, on Mary's twenty-third birthday.

Unlike Mary, Olaf wasn't particularly proud of his ancestors. When you came to America you left your past behind, he often said. He said little more than that he had changed his last name from Nelson to Hasselborg (after his hometown of Hassela) during a stint in the Swedish army.[2] He had completed the equivalent of a few years of college and served a two-year apprenticeship to a master cabinetmaker before coming to America in 1854, at age twenty-nine. By the early 1870s, he had settled in Franconia, a small, prosperous logging town on the St. Croix river about forty miles north of St. Paul. When he met dark-eyed, young Mary Ballard, he was Franconia's postmaster, town clerk, justice of the peace, and tax assessor, besides making an adequate if irregular living as a cabinetmaker.

"Papa was willing [to marry]," Flora wrote in her memoirs, "as he was at an age when most of us want a change of some kind and he was tired of keeping house for himself." On 18 November 1876, less than a year after their marriage, the couple's first child was born. Mary named him Allen, after one of her brothers; Olaf, for reasons he didn't disclose, picked Emmanuel as a middle name.

So it was that Allen Hasselborg came into the world thirteen years after the end of the Civil War, during the heyday of the American cowboy, when the West was almost won. Only about a

Hasselborg house, Franconia, Minnesota, 1880s, with Mr. and Mrs.
Hasselborg and three of their daughters in front (a neighborhood friend is
leaning on the gate). *Courtesy of E. Gardner*

month earlier, the U.S. Army had terminally disciplined the Sioux
and Cheyenne for their role in the Battle of the Little Big Horn.
The final, frenzied assault on the buffalo was well under way as
new railroads brought thousands of homesteaders out to settle
the Great Plains. At the Centennial Exposition in Philadelphia
that summer, the Industrial Age had been ushered in by Alexander
Graham Bell's demonstration of the first telephone.

In eastern Minnesota, several decades had passed since the
last of the French voyageurs paddled up the St. Croix in birch
bark canoes. Not since the 1860s had Indians been more than an
occasional nuisance. The area around Franconia still had some

forest, but much of it had been logged, and most of the land was taken up by small farms. The local economy was fed mainly by white pine cut upriver and floated down to the local sawmill. There were several other small factories, general stores, two hotels, a restaurant, three saloons, a dairy, flour mill, two black-smiths, a gunsmith, and one doctor for the twenty-five families in town. "Our village was so compact that neighbors with good lungs could almost call to one another all over town," Flora remembered, "and no matter where we were, mama could make us hear her clarion call." There were skating parties on the river in the winter and picnics up on the bluffs in the summertime. A favorite pastime was going down to the steamboat landing to watch the lumberjacks break up logjams with dynamite. On election day, all the men voted Republican and drank too much. Attitudes toward the law were relaxed; one of the Hasselborgs' cousins was a case in point. A fat and jolly blacksmith who liked his liquor, Cousin Nels occasionally landed in jail, where he stayed only as long as it took him to pick the lock. After one such episode, he came for dinner at the Hasselborgs with the lock in his pocket and went swaggering off into the night singing what Flora later described as "a ribald song of his own composing."

Cousin Nels's invitation to dine at the Hasselborgs on that occasion probably came from Olaf, not Mary. Olaf did what he pleased most of the time, with little concern for the opinions of others. He liked working in his shop, making furniture and everything from violins to coffins; he sharpened saws and repaired clocks and almost anything else that needed fixing. But he wasn't much interested in making money, and what he made he tended to spend on himself.

"He didn't like physical fighting but liked a verbal battle where the adversary was beaten, right or wrong," Flora recalled. "He was arrogant in his opinions, had a bad temper and worse manners, loved books, flowers and himself." Firmly believing that one could learn anything on one's own, given enough time and intelligence, he subscribed to *Scientific American*, kept a precise daily record of the weather, collected natural history specimens, and grew a flower and vegetable garden that was the envy of his neighbors. If Olaf Hasselborg mispronounced the name of a local wildflower, everyone in Franconia mispronounced it. Often rude to customers at the post office, he refused to help them stamp their letters in the winter when their hands were too cold to do it themselves.

It was just as typical of Allen's mother that she always offered to help. If on a winter night a neighbor got drunk and passed out on the street, she made sure someone brought him in to sleep it off on her kitchen floor. She was well-liked and respected, an efficient housekeeper who worked sixteen hours most days. "Every Monday she washed, even when the sheets froze on the line faster than she could hang them out," Flora remembered. "Our neighbors checked their calendars by her wash on the line. On Tuesday she ironed; Wednesday she mended; Thursday she caught up with odd chores or sewed; Friday she scrubbed; and Saturday she baked cookies and nine big loaves of bread and sometimes cinnamon rolls or coffee cake."

After Allen, Mary would give birth to seven more children in twelve years. In between raising babies and all her other chores, she kept boarders, taught school for the younger children in town, and helped at the post office. About the time her fourth child was born, Olaf remarked, with typical callousness, that she "looked as if she'd been buried six months and dug up." Though Olaf was often nasty to her, Mary always kept her temper and they rarely quarreled, not openly anyway. He liked to drink, too, and it didn't take much for it to go to his head. Mary put up with his drinking

Allen Hasselborg's sisters, c. 1890. Left to right: Pansy, Flora, Ebba (center foreground), and Nellie. *Courtesy of E. Gardner*

most of the time, though on one occasion she marched down to his favorite saloon and told the proprietor never to serve Mr. Hasselborg liquor again.

Yet despite Olaf's meanness, his drinking, and grumpy self-centeredness, from Flora's memoirs comes a picture of a contented family: walks together in the woods on Sundays, winter evenings when the girls sang and danced in the parlor to the tune of Olaf's violin, Christmases when they had a big tree hung with popcorn and frosted animal cookies, and Mary knitted mittens for everybody, and the girls were given china dolls and the boys got knives. "Our house was as good as any in town," Flora remembered. It had a formal parlor, a big kitchen, a library, and Olaf's wood shop on the first floor; three bedrooms on the second floor with a roomy attic above them; and a cellar where Mary stored barrels and jars of fruit and vegetable preserves. "We always had plenty to eat, as good clothes as the neighbors' children, and, in fact, we were among the social elite."

That sense of being among the social elite underlay much of how the Hasselborgs saw themselves and were seen in Franconia. Olaf was an educated, skilled craftsman who held several important civic positions; Mary was well-respected and one of the only American-born women in a town full of European immigrants. So it was with confidence in his own social standing, and with a certain aloofness, that Allen first learned to view people outside his own family. He was further set apart by his father's indifference to him. Olaf often said that his children gave him a headache, particularly his two oldest boys, Allen and Horace. As the first-born son, Allen took the brunt of that resentment, and his overworked mother could do little to help. In Flora's memoirs, he seems always to be off somewhere, remote, veiled. "Sometimes in the evening after school we played ghost," she remembered. "Allen was always the ghost, wrapped in a sheet."

By the time he was in his teens, Allen was spending much of his time alone, hunting in the woods and fields around Franconia, often bringing squirrels, grouse, and rabbits home to the family dinner table. "I knew every trail for miles and most every tree worth knowing for nuts, squirrels, ect.," he would say many years later.[3] "We used to go out in snowstorms and try to get lost but I never could."[4] With a few boys his age, he built wigwams and camped out in rock caves on the hill behind town. The first time he earned some money selling fish, he spent it on a natural history book, and he read the family copy of *Swiss Family Robinson* so many times he nearly wore it out.

And he had a certain fierceness about him. Many years later, he would boast that when one of his teachers in Franconia threatened to whip him, he kicked her in the shins and she backed down.[5] Yet he was also among the brightest students in school and usually won most of the prizes at the end of the year. Shy, intense, and given to sudden fits of anger, he didn't make friends easily. Like many lonely boys growing up in the country, he sought the company of pet animals. The year he turned thirteen, he tamed a male raccoon and kept it until it got too wild, and he had to let it go.

Quick and strong from so much time outdoors and with his mother's dark good looks, he began to attract the attention of girls his own age. He tried to pretend he didn't notice, acting detached and arrogant like his father, but they saw right through him. They teased him, calling him "Your Royal Highness," which only made him withdraw further.[6] He was "mortally afraid" of girls, Flora remembered, even Franconia girls he had known all his life.

In the fall of 1890, the year he turned fourteen, he dropped out of school, explaining to his parents that he had read all the books in the school library and was afraid he might start "retrograding." The following spring he got a job running a ferry across the St. Croix, and with the money he earned, built a pretty canvas canoe that everyone in town admired. The next two years he worked in a logging camp kitchen and on a nearby farm, digging potatoes. By then, steamboat traffic on the river had fallen off due to competition from the St. Paul-Duluth railroad. The first symptoms of a nationwide economic depression were beginning to surface in Franconia; some of the Hasselborgs' neighbors were talking about selling out and moving on.

Early one evening in July 1893, the Hasselborgs' house caught fire. Mary rushed in and made her way up to the second floor, where she was seen pushing smoking mattresses out a window. Neighbors ran over and managed to rescue most of the furniture, but the house and everything else in it went up in smoke. Soon word went around that the fire had started in the attic where Mr. Hasselborg kept his old newspapers, and that the old man had recently filed an insurance claim on the house. Then it became known that he planned to use the insurance money to buy land on the coast of Florida. More than one neighbor put two and two together and Olaf didn't deny their conclusion. For years they had been hearing him say that Florida was the Garden of Eden and that hell wasn't hot, it was as cold as a Minnesota winter.

Flora's memoirs don't say much about how the family responded to Olaf's news, though Mary must have been shocked. It was bad enough that her husband had started the fire, yet here he was at the age of sixty-seven telling her she had to rip her family up by its roots and move more than a thousand miles away to a place none of them had seen before. And she was a Northerner; although she had been only eight when the Civil War began, several Ballard relatives had fought for the Union. Now Olaf was expecting her to start all over on a bayou in the deep South.

Flora remembered that Allen was eager to see the world beyond Minnesota. Soon after the fire, he bought a new rifle and began talking about all the deer he would shoot in Florida. While out practicing with it one day, he shot a neighbor's calf, and had to pay its owner, Ole Andersen, five dollars in damages. Though he promptly apologized, explaining that he had pulled the trigger by mistake, he would admit many years later that in fact his finger had been quite firm on the trigger and he had made what he described as "a good running shot at two hundred yds. measured range."[7] More than likely he was hurt and angry as he drew a bead on that galloping calf, for it was Ole Andersen who had just bought the burned-out remains of the Hasselborgs' house, the only home Allen had ever known, the home his father had just destroyed.

3

OUTCAST IN

FLORIDA

AFTER THE FIRE, the Hasselborgs lived
for several months on the second floor of the post office.[1] Toward
the middle of October 1893, after a going-away party given by
their neighbors, they loaded a wagon with their few remaining
possessions and soon were swaying past the burnt-out remains of
their house, headed for the train station in Taylors Falls.

They traveled first to St. Paul, so Mary could say good-bye to
her relatives, and then to Chicago, where the Columbian
Exposition was attracting visitors from all over the world. The
Hasselborgs didn't attend, although Allen did manage to slip off
to Montgomery Wards to buy ammunition for his new rifle. And
then when they had rattled south for many days and nearly a
thousand miles, he saw salt water for the first time—the Gulf
of Mexico. After a rough trip east along the coast in a freight
schooner, they docked in St. Andrew. Too shy to eat in the hotel
dining room that night, Allen stayed in his room and ate leftovers
from the family picnic basket. The next morning, as they were

Post Office, Franconia, Minnesota, 1880s. Olaf Hasselborg is on the balcony. He was Franconia's postmaster from c. 1880 to 1893. *Courtesy of E. Gardner*

getting ready to take a boat down St. Andrew Bay to their new homestead, he wandered off and had to be picked up later. Thus from the moment he arrived in Florida, he seemed lost and confused, a small-town boy dazed by his strange new life.

It didn't help pick up his spirits when Olaf's eighty acres of paradise turned out to be mostly brush and a few oaks and palmetto palms pushed up against a marshy bayou. The log cabin advertised as an "improvement" by the previous owner was a dilapidated, one-room shack with a leaky roof, a dirt and stick chimney, and one small window. The other improvements amounted to a few beehives and semi-tame razorback hogs, some mite-infested chickens, and an old gray cat.

Olaf and Allen quickly got to work on a new house, and by the next spring, with plum trees, grape vines, and a vegetable garden in the front yard, it looked almost like their place in Minnesota. They made it through the summer without too much trouble: Olaf took a few small carpentry jobs, Mary worked part-time at a nearby store, and Allen and Horace contributed some money they made working on a fishing boat.

By the end of their first year in Florida, however, Olaf's dream had become a nightmare for all of them. They had exhausted their savings and were eating mostly cornbread and too much fish, and getting so they didn't mind the taste of gopher and turtle meat. The plum trees in the front yard had shriveled and died, and only a few scrawny sweet potatoes had survived in the sandy soil. On Christmas Day 1894, they had no tree and no presents, though Mary cooked a chicken for dinner as a special treat. It began raining hard in January, and before they knew what hit them they had been battered and badly scared by a hurricane. Right about then, Olaf stopped looking for work and took to hobbling around on crutches, complaining about his rheumatism. Mary wrote her father in Chicago asking for a loan, but one of her sisters intercepted the letter and scolded her for asking for money she couldn't repay. When she asked the local storekeeper for credit, he turned her down. Mary cried on the way home from the store that day, the only time her children saw her so hurt and humiliated.

It was as if the Hasselborgs had fallen into a deep, dark hole and couldn't climb out. They had left Minnesota winters behind, but they had also left the warmth and security of a community where they had been surrounded by neighbors and relatives, where Olaf had always been able to make money when he felt like it, and they had always had the post office and Mary's boarders and school to fall back on. Now they were two miles from the nearest neighbor and a long boat ride away from St. Andrew, the closest town of any size. In Franconia, Mary's American pedigree and Olaf's education qualified them as "among the social elite"; now they were "Yankees," northerners living on the outskirts of a town nearly destroyed by Union gunships during the Civil War. If in Franconia they had kept somewhat apart, now their neighbors kept apart from them—not that they had any particular desire to socialize. "We Hasselborgs were an alien breed and never could fit," Flora remarked years later. "We never could conform or quite belong to the neighbors."

Anyway, it was hard to imagine keeping company with the disorderly mix of drifters and dreamers, down-and-out artists, land speculators, retired Union soldiers and backwoods "crackers" of uncertain means living on Pitts Bayou. Many of them talked strangely, for one thing, saying "fust" for "first," "tote" for "carry" and "how do you come on" when they said hello. Entire families, adults and children alike, took snuff, smoked tobacco, and played the fiddle. The women all wore nightgowns under their skirts and palm frond hats. For many of them, marriage seemed to be an afterthought, if it occurred at all, and there was often some question as to whose children belonged to whom. Customers at the store where Mary worked, when reminded of bills past due, challenged the owner to duels. Few of them paid much attention to the law.

With Olaf now fully retired, the full weight of supporting the family fell on Mary and the older children. Though in her mid-forties, with her children to worry about, Mary was as resolute as ever. She helped set up a post office in a nearby village so she could make money working there, and often sat up late into the night knitting fishing nets they could sell. Allen and Horace tried to help by contributing the money they made fishing in the spring and fall, but it wasn't much. Nellie, the oldest girl, taught school, and the other girls occasionally did housework for neighbors in exchange for room and board; even Ebba and Ira, the youngest two, pitched in, picking blackberries and helping Mary dig oysters at the mouth of the bayou. But it wasn't enough. They never could afford new clothes and had to depend on relatives in Minnesota for hand-me-downs that never fit. The children went barefoot most of the year, though Mary now and then could afford to make canvas shoes for them.

To make matters worse, Olaf's mind began slipping away. In the winter he sat in the kitchen warming his feet in the oven; in the summer he sat by a front window most of the day, except when he took a nap. When he cooked fish in the oven, he always forgot them and burned them to a crisp. Once he cooked up an alligator head just to see what it would look like. Convinced they were all going to starve, he began hoarding pancakes in an old chest where he kept an odd assortment of broken clocks and other personal treasures. He would forget about them, and they would mold, and Mary would have to throw them out when he wasn't looking. The more he deteriorated, the meaner he was to his children. When Allen's sisters invited friends over, he drove them away. Once he insulted Flora so badly she picked up an iron poker and was about to bash him on the head with it before Mary stopped her. Furious, Flora informed her mother that if her father ever said anything like that to her again, she would kill him and no one could stop her. He was a hateful old man and deserved to die, she screamed. What right did he have to be so mean when he had dragged them down to Florida in the first place? Why had her mother ever married him? Flora wanted to know. Mary sadly told her that she hadn't known Olaf very well to begin with and that he had gotten much worse over the years.

As always, Olaf was hardest on his eldest son, criticizing him constantly for not finding a job. Allen tried to get work, but other than fishing, there was none to be had. Even when he did chores around the homestead, Olaf always found fault with him. Then Mary began fainting and had to take to her bed for two or three days at a time. During one of her worst spells, she called Allen to her bedroom and told him to take care of the family when she was gone.

In Franconia Allen had been shy, though independent and rebellious at times. Now, in his late teens, fighting constantly with his father, burdened by his mother's dependence on him, depressed and paralyzed with uncertainty about himself, he withdrew even further. He would sit alone for hours in his room reading old catalogs and magazines, mope around the homestead catching chickens with a grain of corn tied on a string, or hunt alligators with two middle-aged bachelors who lived nearby. His sisters and mother tried to bring him out of it, but they were afraid of prodding him too hard—he always seemed ready to explode. Highly judgmental and moralistic, he was fiercely defensive of his sisters, on one occasion strongly objecting to one of their beaux whose mother had left her husband for another man. He thought his mother trusted men too much, especially all the old reprobates in St. Andrew who liked to seduce innocent young girls. When his mother expressed strong support for the Spanish-American War, he argued hotly with her, calling it "a war on paper" and scoffing at the thirteen dollars a month the government was offering as soldier's pay. "It was too bad he didn't go," Flora said later. "Maybe he'd have gotten used to people and over being afraid of women."

In the spring of 1898, he worked his way up the coast on a schooner to Pensacola and headed north. By the first of July, he was in Franconia. Unable to find a job, he camped out in the woods, at one point treating some friends to pancakes enriched with turtle eggs. At the Fourth of July town picnic, he caused quite a ruckus after his cousin Nels, the jolly blacksmith, got him drunk on beer and he soundly thrashed three men who were bothering him. Shortly thereafter, he was in St. Paul working at a livery stable owned by one of his Ballard uncles. The pay wasn't good, though, and his aunt made him run errands for her, so he caught a train back to Florida. When he got home, his family was shocked to see that his only suit still had bloodstains from his July Fourth brawl.

That winter, a big snowstorm hit western Florida and the temperature dropped to two above zero. The next thing his family knew, Allen was out in Arizona in a mining town. Like Horace, who had gone north the year before, he left without saying good-bye. No doubt he was looking for work, and he was escaping Olaf and the emptiness of his life in Florida. He would say later that he ran away from home.[2] But was he running toward something? Did he have a destination in mind? Judging by the direction he took, north and west, and given that in a letter he wrote to Flora a few months later he mentioned the Klondike gold rush, it seems probable that like thousands of other men all over the world that year, he was headed for Alaska, dreaming of striking it rich.[3]

4

NORTHBOUND

WRITING HIS FAMILY several months after leaving home, Allen was a little lonely ("write soon and tell me all of the news") but, at the age of twenty-two, clearly thrilled to be on his own. He had found work at a copper mine in Clifton, Arizona, keeping the tailings out of the river in front of the smelter. "There isent enough water in the river to wash it away so we are hauling it off," he explained. He wasn't sure how long his job would last, as the river was expected to rise in a few weeks, but he planned to stick with it as long as he could. Most of the other mine workers were Mexican, so he was trying to learn Spanish. It was "pretty rough country." A baseball game had broken up after shots were fired over the pitcher's head, and all the cowboys and miners in town had revolvers and Bowie knives in their belts. "There has been three men killed since I have been here," he reported. "I was well acquainted with one." He signed that first letter, "Your Big Bad Bro Allen."[1]

By the middle of June, the temperature in Clifton during the day was more than a hundred degrees in the shade. Allen had been working hard, eighty-six of the ninety-three days since he arrived. He was making only about thirty-five dollars a month, much less than if he worked at the smelter, but he said the men there got sick from the sulfur fumes and usually could only work half-time. For the time being, he was content to be earning enough to pay his room and board and still have some left over to send to his mother. The boarding house served good food and plenty of it. He teased his sisters with a detailed description of the menu:

> For breakfast we have mush, 2 eggs, our choice
> of 2 or 3 kinds of meat and 2 hot cakes besides
> bread potatoes and buttermilk coffee sugar ect. For
> dinner soup, 2 kinds of mush, potatoes, 2 kinds of
> vegetables, pudding and pie. For supper 2 kinds
> of meat 2 kinds of vegs, sauce or fruit and cake. I
> don't like the board at all. I cant hardly eat it.[2]

A few weeks later, he was working nights, trying to save money by sleeping in a hay shed during the day. With all the flies and the terrible heat, he was thinking about paying for a room again, though Clifton was booming now and everything was more expensive. On July Fourth, a small glass of weak lemonade had sold for ten cents, he told Flora. Things cost as much as they did in the Klondike![3] He mentioned the Klondike casually, as if his family already knew he might be headed there, so they may not have been too surprised when he wrote next from a schooner anchored off the Shumagin Islands in western Alaska. It was the middle of November 1899.

> It is a tough, dirty, stinking hole where I am
> sitting writing this letter in the forcastle. The[re]
> are 13 of us down here and it haint bigger than a
> bedroom at home. We are a queer mixed up crowd.
> There are 2 norwegians 2 portuguese 1 swede 1
> dane 1 russian 1 german 1 hollander 1 austrian 1
> englishman 1 canadian 1 californian 1 new yorker
> and myself.[4]

Clifton, Arizona, 1903. *Courtesy of Arizona Historical Society*

What he didn't mention was that he had not made the trip to Alaska entirely of his own volition. He had gone to Seattle and was working odd jobs around the docks, looking for cheap passage north, when someone knocked him out and threw a bag over his head. By the time he woke up he was on the *Arago*, an eighty-ton fishing vessel, and well out to sea. It turned out that the rest of the crew had been shanghaied, too, and they all were bound, willy-nilly, for a winter of codfishing in the Bering Sea. He would say many years later that he hadn't really minded getting kidnapped like that—he was headed for Alaska anyway.[5]

Writing his family now, he allowed as how he wasn't going to make much money fishing because he was expected to pay for his own food, clothes, and outfit. He might try to go to the gold country in the spring, he said, though that was just a possibility, not a definite plan. He was still more than a thousand miles from the gold fields and had heard that most of the best claims had already been staked. Ahead of him were four or five months of grueling work, fishing from a dory, fighting heavy seas day after day, baiting and setting hand lines in bitter cold weather, pulling in cod and halibut weighing hundreds of pounds. At night he labored long hours on deck, cleaning and salting fish. The rest of his time was spent packed into the "dirty, stinking" forecastle with the rest of the "queer, mixed-up" crew. And then when the *Arago* docked in Seattle, the captain kept half his pay. His shipmates got him drunk and robbed him of the rest.[6] He didn't report his embarrassing return to his family. He was Big Bad Bro Allen, after all. When he wrote home in July 1900, he just said he had used octopus for bait and that while there wasn't much money in cod fishing, he had liked it "first rate."[7]

By then he was fishing on the Columbia River with his brother, Horace, living with eighteen other men and twelve horses on a big barge tied up near Skamokawa, Washington, about twenty-five miles in from the coast. Most mornings they got up at three and worked until ten at night, loading nets onto barges that were towed into the river, then hitching up horses to haul the nets back in. One of the nets was eight hundred yards long and sixty feet deep. On a good day, they made six sets and caught four thousand pounds of chinook salmon and steelhead. Compared to fishing on the *Arago,* it was fairly easy, and Allen was happy to be making two dollars a day.[8] The job ended in August, though. Horace left for Florida, and Allen was alone again, killing time in Astoria, Oregon. By late fall, he was back in Alaska. He had found work, "terrible hard work," he said, in one of the Treadwell mines, near Juneau.[9]

"I am working down in the mine breaking rock and pushing ore cars. I get $2.00 per day and board. I have been on night shift two weeks. It dont make any difference to us though whether it is day or night. We have to work by candlelight anyway."[10]

Pushing ore carts was brute labor; breaking rock was just as hard, but required much more skill. In a cramped chamber several hundred feet underground, for eight hours at a stretch, he shoveled ore down a chute to carts hauling it out to be processed. A "grizzly"—three twelve-foot steel bars spaced about thirty inches apart—lay over the top of the ore chute. If a chunk was too big to fit through, he blasted it down to size with dynamite. It was dangerous, nerve-wracking work. The dynamite was touchy, tunnels occasionally caved in, and there was always the risk of poisonous gas. That winter, even when he worked the day shift, dawn was just breaking when he went into the mine and it was dark by the time he emerged in midafternoon. "After we quit work all we think of is supper and going to bed," he told Flora.[11]

One of the largest hardrock gold mining operations in the world, the Treadwell Company had recently doubled its production capacity. The year 1900 would be its best ever. The adjoining towns of Treadwell and Douglas bustled with activity, and across Gastineau Channel, Juneau was also feeling its oats. A ramshackle mining camp twenty years earlier, it had just been declared the capital of the territory. Money was coming into all three towns from a number of local mines, lumber mills, and salmon-curing operations. They could now boast about having electric light, telephones, paved streets, and all the necessary services and conveniences of respectable communities in the states: hotels, newspapers, a hospital, a bank, nine general stores, a theater, and more than enough doctors and lawyers to go around. Less a matter of civic pride were the dozens of saloons, breweries, dance halls, and other bawdy establishments doing a brisk business on both sides of the channel.

Allen Hasselborg, Astoria, Oregon, 1900. "I have just got some pictures from the gallery so will write you enclosing a half dozen. I don't suppose you will be satisfied with them as I haven't got a white shirt on. I guess you won't like my necktie neither." *Allen Hasselborg, letter to his family with photographs enclosed. Courtesy of Alaska Historical Library*

Despite such possible diversions, Allen Hasselborg apparently kept pretty much to himself that winter. In letters to his family, he made no mention of friends or a social life of any kind. His job was hard, his hardest yet, and he didn't have time or energy for anything else. By February, after working in the cold, damp mine for almost five months, his joints hurt so much he decided to leave Alaska, though he didn't want to.[12]

Within a month, he was down in Prescott, Arizona, lured by the possibility of another mining job. Once again, his plans didn't work out:

> I havent got any steady work yet and mean to leave this town today. There isent enough work around here for the people who live here. . . . I got a job in one mine and worked 3 days, then the manager came and stopped the work and laid most of us off. I worked in a machine shop all last week but the man whose place I was working in came back today so I am out of a job again. You will be apt to hear from me in Oregon or Alaska in a month or so. I'll stay when I get there this time I guess.[13]

And so he bounced thousands of miles back north again, determined to make a go of it in Alaska. By the middle of August, he and a partner were gillnetting salmon in Taku Inlet, about twenty miles south of Juneau. It was the toughest fishing he had ever done, he told his family, and they were getting only five cents apiece for their fish. The water was full of huge icebergs, some more than an acre across and thirty feet tall, which tore up their nets and constantly threatened to sink their boat.[14] By September, he had made eighty-five dollars and was hoping to make more, though the weather was turning bad and the fishing wouldn't last much longer.[15] A month later, after attempting to find work in one of the Juneau mines, he left to spend the winter of 1902 chopping wood and clearing brush at the site for a new fort the army was building in Haines.[16]

In 1903 he was working at a mine on Baranof Island when he heard that his father had died. His response was a terse note to his mother: "I'm sorry Papa is dead. I'll send some money as soon as I can."[17] That fall, he went to Sitka and built a dory. In November, when he knew he might have to contend with snow, high winds, and rough seas, he set out to row the eighty miles to Juneau. His route took him down Peril Strait, around the southern tip of Admiralty Island, and up to the head of Seymour Canal, where he dragged his boat a mile overland to Oliver Inlet. It was January by the time he pulled the final ten miles into town.[18]

By then he was determined to stay in Alaska. He had burst free from his family with enough force to send him ricocheting back and forth between Alaska and the states three times in two years, drifting about thirteen thousand miles, not spending more than a few months in one place. Like other footloose young men who came to Alaska in the early 1900s, he had been running from poverty and an unhappy home toward adventure and a chance to prove himself.

The prevailing mood of optimism in Alaska may have also encouraged him to stay. The population of the territory had more than doubled during the Klondike and Nome gold rushes, and, as a result, the federal government, after neglecting Alaskans for several decades, had begun to give them more of a say in their own affairs. By 1903, Congress had made it somewhat easier for them to own land and had instituted a preliminary form of civil government. Although the land laws were far more restrictive than similar laws in the states and the new civil code wasn't much more than a first step, many Alaskans were confident that the wealth of the territory was about to be unlocked.

For Allen Hasselborg, however, it was more than just economic opportunity, real or imagined, that brought him to roost in south-eastern Alaska; it went beyond the distance he had put between himself and his life in Florida. While fishing Taku Inlet in 1901, and during his winter in Haines, he had had his first glimpse of the country outside Juneau. On his row from Sitka, he had seen range upon range of unexplored mountains and forests that seemed to go on forever. By now an experienced hunter, trapper, and fisherman, he had found everything he wanted, all in the same vast, wild place.

After 1904, he was always out on his own, living off the land—fishing, trapping, and prospecting. And it was during those years that he shot his first Alaska brown bear. He would tell a friend years later that brown bears were so scarce and wary when he first came to Alaska, he hunted off and on for four years before he even saw one.[19]

With the dramatic growth of Alaska's population at the turn of the century, brown bears had been hard hit. Until 1902, when Congress passed the territory's first Comprehensive Game Law, there had been no hunting regulations protecting any wild game animals in Alaska. While the new laws gave bears a small measure of protection by prohibiting hunting between April 15 and July 1, limiting each hunter to four bears per year, and banning the export of hides that weren't scientific specimens or sport trophies, enforcement was almost nonexistent. Alaskans protested the ban on the export of hides so vociferously that Congress removed it in 1904. By then, most brown bears in southeastern had learned to avoid the beaches, where they were most vulnerable to hunters. Even in midsummer, Hasselborg often had to go three or four thousand feet into the mountains to find them.[20] But it was well worth the effort. A hide in good condition sold for as much as fifty dollars in Juneau,[21] more than

Northern pike caught near Yakutat by
Allen Hasselborg, his .45/70 Winchester and
12-gauge shotgun in background.
Courtesy of Sheppard family

he could make in a month of fishing or working in a mine, and he
could combine bear hunting with other work—keep an eye out
and his rifle handy while prospecting in the mountains or fishing
near shore.

It was Alaska coastal brown bears he was after, a breed apart from the grizzlies of interior Alaska and the rest of North America. Not much was known about them, though their range was thought to be the narrow band of mountains along the coast of Alaska from the southeastern panhandle north to Kodiak Island. In early spring, after emerging from their dens high in the mountains, they fed on new vegetation and roots, usually on south-facing slopes. By May, some were down lower scavenging dead deer and other carrion left by the winter, while others were already at sea level, grazing on salty grass in the tide meadows. In early August, when the hunting season opened, Hasselborg might find a few lurking along the more secluded salmon streams and beaches, but usually he had to go up into the forest after them.

He walked slowly, cautiously, trying to make no sudden movement and no sound as he pushed through thick brush, climbed over tumbled piles of wind-felled trees and across steep slopes littered with slippery, rotting logs. Except for an occasional bird call or the chattering of a squirrel, the forest was very still. The bears could slip silently through the undergrowth, so he had to be alert to the slightest movement anywhere around him. On an overcast or rainy day, the light was dim and flat; when sunlight slanted down through the trees, harsh shadows played tricks with his eyes. And because bears could smell humans coming as much as a half a mile away, he had to be aware of the direction of every breeze.

Seldom did he catch a bear by surprise, and it was all too easy to be almost on top of one before he saw it. Sometimes they ran off; other times they watched him approach, as if asking to be shot; now and then one would challenge him, running fast towards him and stopping short when it saw him or caught his scent. Often all he could see at first was a pair of beady eyes watching him over the top of a log, or a mosaic of dark brown shapes

Brown bear, Admiralty Island, late 1920s. From *The Wild Grizzlies of Alaska*, by John M. Holzworth. *Courtesy of G. P. Putnam's Sons*

blurred by the foliage. Rarely did he have time to wait until the bear turned broadside and he could take proper aim at the shoulder or just behind it. The most important thing was to knock them down so they couldn't run, as it usually took at least two shots from his .45/70 to kill them. If they didn't go down and ran off into heavy cover, he had his work cut out for him; they never bled much, so they were hard to track. And it was almost always the wounded ones that attacked. He would have no more than a second or two to aim and fire. Faster than a racehorse out of a starting gate, they came for him in great leaping bounds, as much as a dozen feet at a time, head low to the ground, ears flat against their heads, wailing and bawling loudly, a terrifying, unearthly sound if you weren't used to it. It took the cool nerves and agility of an athlete to face a charging bear and make each shot count.

Most hunts were pretty routine, though. Some were like shooting a cow in a meadow. Though he loaded soft-point bullets that delivered a blow of more than a ton, they often refused to die quickly. He shot one bear three times, once in the heart, and still it turned a somersault and ran a hundred and fifty feet before collapsing; another one fell only after taking seven slugs in its heart and lungs.[22] Afterward, he might be an hour or two taking the hide, as he had to skin out the skull and each paw down to the claws carefully and split the ears, nose, and lips to remove all the cartilage. Leaving the huge, pink carcass where it lay, he tied the hide firmly to his pack frame; it might weigh as much as a hundred and fifty pounds, a heavy load to carry through the forest and freight back to camp in a dory. And still the hunt wasn't really over until he had scraped and salted the skin and stretched it out to dry.

It was hard work, but he was his own boss and he was good at it, very good. Toughened by years of hard physical labor and outdoor living, a crack shot and avid explorer who liked nothing better than hunting wild country on his own, it was as if all his life he had been preparing to hunt bears, and now here he was, shy kid from Minnesota, poor boy from the bayous, Big Bad Bro Allen up in Alaska, slaying the dragon of the dark woods over and over again.

5

THE BEST

WOODSMAN

ON A SPRING DAY in the middle of May 1907, Hasselborg rowed out of a small bay near Mole Harbor and turned north up Seymour Canal. Piled in his dory were a brown bear hide and a beaver carcass he hoped to sell to some scientists camped at Windfall Harbor, about twenty miles away. It had been a hard winter on Admiralty Island, with freezing temperatures and roaring winds that kept him holed up most of the time, unable to do much fishing. Now spring had finally arrived. Though patches of snow were still visible behind the beach, the alder had begun to leaf out and the soft hooting of blue grouse drifted faintly out to him over the water.[1]

As he rowed through the pass between Windfall Island and Late Point, he spotted the white tents of the Alexander Expedition on the far side of the bay. One imagines the bow of his dory crunching into the beach, Hasselborg stepping out, the Californians coming down to greet him. No doubt they were delighted with the bear hide and beaver, and Hasselborg was just

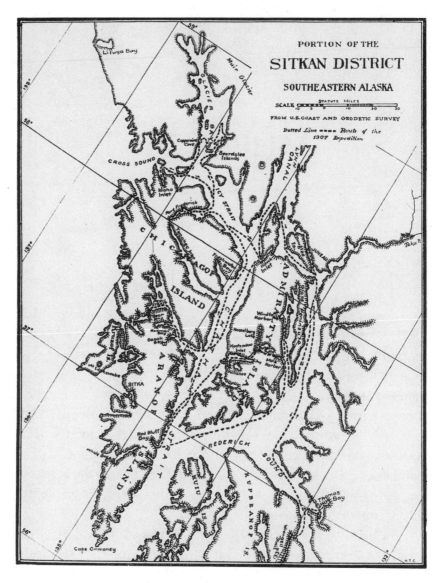

Map of the region traveled by the 1907 Alexander Alaska Expedition.
The dotted line shows the route of the expedition.
Courtesy of Alaska Historical Library

as pleased to meet them; they had all kinds of fancy equipment and guns, and obviously meant business.[2] Chase Littlejohn, middle-aged and portly, had hunted bear in the Aleutians. Mr. and Mrs. Frank Stephens, an older couple from San Diego, were both experienced naturalists. Joseph Dixon, a biology student at Stanford University, was keenly interested in wildlife and enthusiastic about almost everything else. And then there was Anne Alexander, the sponsor and leader of the expedition, in her late thirties, daughter of a wealthy San Francisco businessman, zealous amateur naturalist and crack shot who had hunted big game in Africa. She had come to Alaska at the request of Dr. C. Hart Merriam, the director of the U.S. Biological Survey, who for several years had been trying to classify the various species of North American bears. Needing more specimens from Alaska, he had introduced Alexander to Joseph Grinnell, an ornithologist determined to secure bird specimens from the islands near Juneau. The two of them had agreed to organize an expedition together. Grinnell would stay behind in California and serve as the expedition's principal scientific adviser, while Alexander went north with four other naturalists for a summer of exploration and collecting in southeastern Alaska.

Arriving in Juneau on April 14, they had traveled by launch to Windfall Harbor and had quickly gone to work. "We fired into a flock of about a dozen waders the other day and picked up four Aleutian sandpipers, a black turnstone and a surfbird," Dixon reported to Grinnell a few days later.[3] Two or three feet of snow in the woods behind the beach had kept them hunting mostly along the water's edge, however, and while they secured a few shorebirds, ducks, small mammals, and bald eagles, they had yet to shoot a bear; they hadn't even seen a track. The bears had just emerged from their dens, and were still high in the mountains, feeding on deer killed by the hard winter. Since they hadn't thought to bring snowshoes, the Californians couldn't go up after them.[4]

Some Tlingits camped on Windfall Island had offered a different explanation for the expedition's lack of success. "One old squaw came over the other day and we finally got her to talk English," Dixon told Grinnell. "She said: 'Bear be heap smart, he hear gun, he no come. You white men damned fools. Shoot! Shoot!! Shoot!!! all the time.' It seems to be beyond their thick heads to imagine what we want with the little birds. But of course we have to shoot them."[5]

Though several hunters had sold them two bear hides, by the time Hasselborg showed up, they were getting pretty discouraged. It was a relief to talk with the thickset, weather-beaten, young Alaskan who knew so much about southeastern Alaska and brown bears. "Miss Alexander has hired a man by the name of Al Hasselborg to go with us," Dixon wrote happily to Grinnell. "He is an accurate observer and possesses a great deal of local knowledge of the islands and is altogether the best woodsman that I have ever seen."[6]

Because the latest U.S. Government maps of the interior of Admiralty Island showed only a blank space walled off by mountains rising four thousand feet from the sea, Hasselborg's knowledge of the island promised to be particularly valuable. Even the Tlingits, who had lived on it for thousands of years, knew little about it, as they were a coastal people who seldom ventured far inland. To them, the interior was the haunt of dangerous beings, especially Khutz, the brown bear, and the island was xutsnuwu x̱a't, "Brown Bear's Fort Island."[7]

Alexander was particularly interested in Hasselborg's description of several lakes west of Mole Harbor; he had discovered them while prospecting, he said, and as far as he knew, no other white man had seen them. She quickly ordered base camp

Members of 1907 Alexander Expedition holding a bald eagle specimen collected at Windfall Harbor, Admiralty Island. *Courtesy of University of California Museum of Vertebrate Zoology*

moved down to Mole Harbor, and within a few days, they were on their way up to the lakes with Hasselborg in the lead.

Though they were able to follow game trails for short distances, it was tough going most of the time. They had to force their way through thick brush, grappling with devil's club, a tall, spiky plant covered with stinging thorns. All the while they were muscling a canoe and their other equipment over huge logs, under wind-felled trees, and across deep patches of wet snow and mud bogs that sucked at their boots. Though now and then the forest opened up into stands of huge spruce and hemlock trees towering overhead, they were relieved finally to arrive at the first lake and paddle out across the water with wide vistas of mountains all around.

"At the time of our first visit, May 21, the lakes were free of ice," Frank Stephens would write later.

> Apparently this had not long been the case and patches of snow were still plentiful in the surrounding forest, while the higher parts of the mountains were bare only on the ridges exposed to sun and wind. The border of the lakes was a dense forest of spruce and hemlock with some alder and a little willow where the shores were not too steep. The underbrush was very thick and overhung the lake shores, while there was very little beach anywhere.[8]

It took them a week to explore what turned out to be a chain of three lakes. They named the largest after Hasselborg; the second largest after Alexander, and the smallest, Beaver, after an animal they were surprised and delighted to discover there. The beaver were very tame, having seen few if any humans, and they easily collected six. Hasselborg stunned another one, but it woke up and capsized the canoe, and he had to let go of it to save one of the cameras. The few bears they spotted were very wary, and stayed out of reach high above the treeline. Toward the end of the week, they saw three on a snow slide to the west of Hasselborg Lake but by then were low on food and too hungry and tired to hunt.[9]

On the way back down to Mole Harbor, Dixon learned a hard lesson about the mountains of southeastern Alaska. Badly lost, he wandered for hours before stumbling onto the beach just a short distance from camp. "When I tried to get up the next morning I promptly fell over and lay there a while," he wrote Grinnell. "I lay around for two days kind of dazed and kept wanting to walk all the time. Now I keep a compass chained to me all the time but expect to get lost again as Hasselborg and Stephens both had compasses the other day and still missed their way."[10]

Back up at the lakes a few days later, Dixon and Alexander had the pleasure of watching Hasselborg shoot the expedition's first brown bear. Dixon:

> We made camp at about six o'clock, ate supper and then went out in the canoe to look for bear, up on the mountainside. We soon saw one feeding in a gulch and Hasselborg started up after it. Littlejohn went up the creek and Miss Alexander and I watched from the boat and motioned to Hasselborg when the bear moved. Hasselborg had to climb nearly 1000 feet, but part of it was up a snow slide. He made it in 40 minutes. (It took us $1^1/_2$ hours several days afterwards.)
>
> Then we heard six shots and saw the bear disappear into the alders. Pretty soon we heard a dull thump, thump, and the old bear came rolling down over the cliffs. He fell about a quarter of a mile and would have rolled clear to the lake had he not hit a log just right. We skinned him next morning and found that four shots had hit him. . . . The fur was rather poor but the skull was about as large as the largest that we have.[11]

The next day, Hasselborg took Dixon hunting ptarmigan in the mountains above Hasselborg Lake. They hadn't gone far when it began to get steep and they came to several cliffs they couldn't climb. Several times they had to go down a ways or traverse to find a better route. While crossing a rock slide filled with rotten

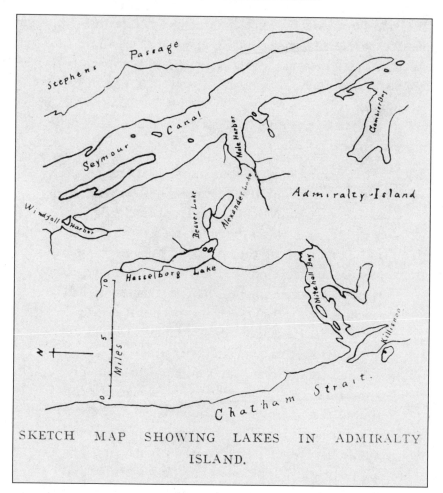

SKETCH MAP SHOWING LAKES IN ADMIRALTY ISLAND.

Map of central area of Admiralty Island lakes drawn by Allen Hasselborg. This map was published in a 1908 issue of *Forest and Stream* magazine. Although no credit for the map accompanied the published article, Allen Hasselborg wrote "map by A. Hasselborg" on his personal copy of the article.

50

snow, Dixon fell through. "I hung onto the gun," he told Grinnell, "and that was all that saved me from being put into cold storage for eternity, as the slides rarely melt. The gun caught on each side of the hole and I did some pretty lively scrambling, I can tell you!"[12]

By the time the two hunters reached the top, it was beginning to snow. Dixon spotted what looked like a pigeon circling around the summit. When it flew closer, he realized it was a ptarmigan, the first of five they would see that day. "They would fly out over the mountain side and let out a rasping cackle which sounds just like someone running a nail over the teeth of a stiff comb," he wrote. "I got three of them."[13]

Back down at Mole Harbor, Alexander decided that Littlejohn and the Stephenses would proceed by launch to Baranof Island while she, Dixon, and Hasselborg explored the river running out of the southern end of Hasselborg Lake. Five days later, Hasselborg wrote his mother from Killisnoo, a Tlingit village on the west side of the island. Big rapids on the upper stretches of the river had worried them at first, he said, and they had to portage through thick timber for about half a mile, but they had floated out through the tide rips in Kootznahoo Inlet less than three days after leaving Mole Harbor. "No one has ever been across this island in a boat before," Hasselborg proudly told his mother. "We carried the canoe over the hills 5 or 6 miles and came down acrost 3 lakes and a big stream."[14] He had killed only two bears since he wrote last, he said, but that didn't matter, since Alexander was now paying him a good salary.

Reunited a few days later on Baranof Island, the expedition motored north up Chatham Strait. The strain of living in close quarters was beginning to take its toll. They were all tired of carrying gear up and down beaches, the launch was filthy, and everyone was irritable, especially Littlejohn, who kept

Allen Hasselborg, Hasselborg Creek, Admiralty Island, June 12, 1907, during historic crossing, Mole Harbor to Killisnoo. *Courtesy of University of California Museum of Vertebrate Zoology*

complaining that he hadn't even shot at a bear yet. By then it was obvious to everyone that his physical condition was not well suited to the rigors of hunting bears, and that Hasselborg was much better at it anyway.

Hasselborg collected three more on Chichagof Island, two of which were a male and female traveling together, a courting pair. After following their tracks all one afternoon and most of the next morning, he shot and wounded the male. The female immediately charged. He killed her with one shot, then went after the male and found it waiting for him under a fallen tree, biting at its wound. He fired and the bear flung itself into the air with a loud roar and landed upright on its hind feet not more than ten feet away—so close he could almost touch it with his rifle. He fired twice more, aiming for the heart. The bear staggered towards him, pawing the air, lunging for him one last time before collapsing.[15]

By early July, they were camped in Glacier Bay and it was raining or trying to most of the time, Dixon reported; everything had mold on it and they were afraid they would start to mold next. Although collecting was going well, they had burned some valuable specimens while trying to dry them on the stove. Things were still a little tense between them. "There is naturaly [*sic*] a lack of centralization in an expedition like this," Dixon wrote. "It took me all morning, the other day, to find out what I was expected to do for the day and finally I was turned loose to do as I pleased. In fact, it is that way about half the time. If I am alone or with Hasselborg I know what to do but when the whole camp is along you have to look out or you are on someone's toes."[16]

Everyone's spirits improved when Hasselborg helped Littlejohn shoot his first bear. After a quick excursion out to shoot seabirds on the Marble Islands, they headed back to Juneau, stopping along the way at Hawk Inlet, on Admiralty Island, to look for bears. Hasselborg soon found a square mile tangled with wind felled trees where about a dozen bears were living. "The bear had been hunted so much they knew just what a man was and were wise accordingly," Dixon wrote.

> Hasselborg killed two. The first one was in the bottom of the creek bed fishing salmon when H. [Hasselborg] saw her first. She was only about 30 feet away through some salmon berry bushes, but 3 shots from the 45-70 put her out of commission.

The other one was not so easy. H. had tracked him from the place in the creek where he had been fishing up to his nest under an upturned tree on the ridge. When H. first saw the bear he was about 75 yards away thru some thick timber. The bear had just his head over a log and was watching Hasselborg.

The first shot hit the bone that surrounds the eye. This caused it to mushroom and leave the jacket. The bullet tore on thru the neck and then turned and went down along the windpipe, thru a lung, cutting a large artery, on thru the intestines and *out* near the hind leg. The bear turned around two or three times then made a bee line down the hill for Hasselborg who kept pumping lead into him. The ground was thickly covered with fallen logs and dead saplings but the bear didn't waste any time dodging among the trees. He meant *business*.

The fifth shot found Hasselborg with an empty gun in his hands and the bear just getting up as the last shot had knocked him down. H. plunged his hand into his pocket and pulled out 4 shells but two of them were wrong end to and he dropped them trying to get them into the magazine. He ran as he loaded but the bear was almost upon him and coming strong. H. took two snap shots at less than 15 feet and then made a flying leap over some logs. The only thing that saved him was that the bear was beginning to get sick and didn't turn and his momentum carried him on down the hill, where he wallowed around a bit then turned up his toes (literally).[17]

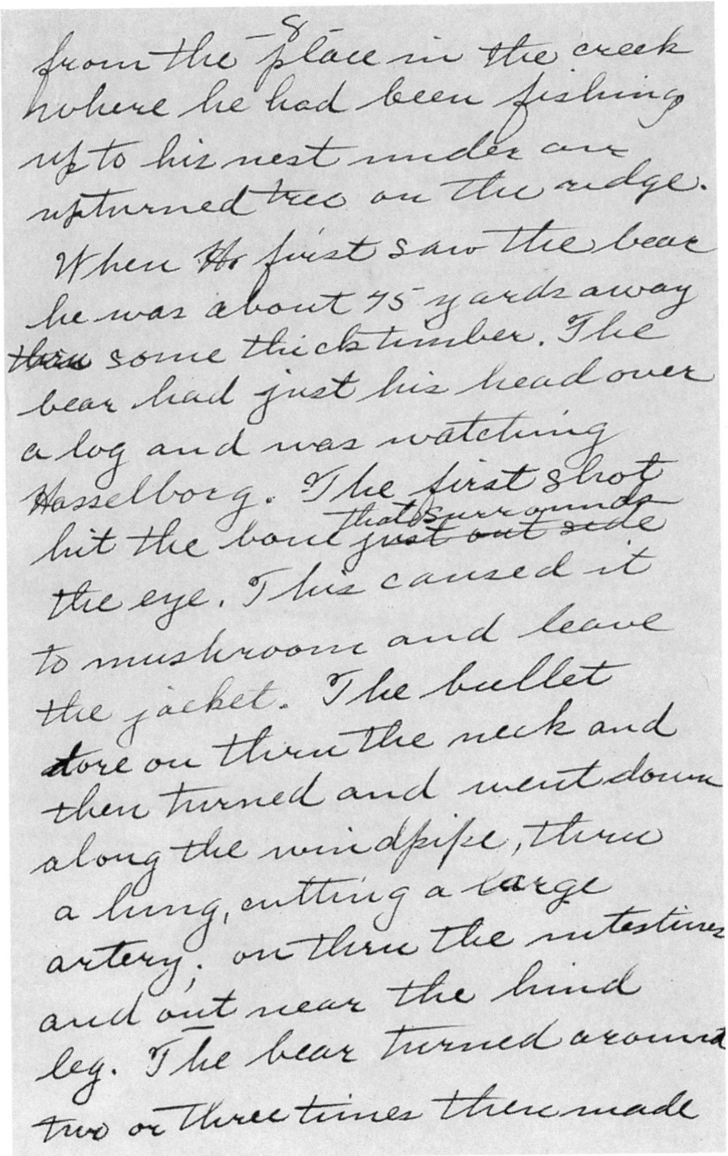

from the place in the creek
where he had been fishing
up to his nest under an
upturned tree on the ridge.
When He first saw the bear
he was about 75 yards away
~~thru~~ some thick timber. The
bear had just his head over
a log and was watching
Hasselborg. The first shot
hit the bone that run around ~~just out side~~
the eye. This caused it
to mushroom and leave
the jacket. The bullet
~~tore~~ on thru the neck and
then turned and went down
along the windpipe, thru
a lung, cutting a large
artery; on thru the intestines
and out near the hind
leg. The bear turned around
~~two~~ or three times then made

A section of text photocopied from Joseph Dixon's letter to Joseph Grinnell, continued on pages 56–57, describing the Hawk Inlet bear hunt during the 1907 Alexander Expedition. *Courtesy of University of California, Berkeley, Bancroft Library*

a bee line down the hill
for Hasselborg who kept
pumping lead into him.
The ground was thickly
covered with fallen logs and
dead saplings but the
bear didn't waste any time
dodging about among the
trees. He meant business.
The fifth shot found
Hasselborg with an empty
gun in his hands and the
bear just getting up as the
last shot had knocked him
down. H. plunged his hand
into his pocket and pulled
out 4 shells but two of them
were wrong end to and he
dropped them trying to
get them into the magazine

he ran as he loaded but the
bear was almost upon him
and coming strong. H. took
two snap shots at less than
15 feet and then made a
flying leap over some logs.
The only thing that saved
him was that the bear was
begining to get sick and didnt
turn and his momentum
carried him on down the
hill where he wallowed
around a bit then turned.
up his toes (literally).

When we skinned him
we found that six out of the
seven bullets had hit him.
They were all 45-70 soft points
backed by smokeless powder.

When they skinned the bear, they found where six of Hasselborg's seven shots had hit. "I had lots of fun carving him up hunting for bullets," Dixon said, "but it was the biggest piece of dissecting that I ever tackled."[18] It was a male, six feet six inches from nose to tail, and not more than three or four years old, as they could cut through one of its ribs with a single swipe of a pocket knife. Dixon took careful measurements: "His neck was just 12 in. thru and his forearm was 20 in. in circumference 2 in. below the elbow. His front paw was 7 in. across the sole and his hind foot was 13 inches long. His intestines were 72 feet long and two inches in diameter."[19]

Writing his family the second week of August, Hasselborg said that before leaving for California, Miss Alexander had left orders for him to keep hunting until October.

> I have killed 7 big brown bear since we were out, and that is considered pretty good. Besides I was busy at other work most of the time. We are going to Rodman Bay [Baranof Island] next but write to me at Juneau. Well I have got our name down on the map. They named the big lake that I discovered on Admiralty Island Hasselborg Lake and the river that comes out of it Hasselborg River. The lake is 10 miles long and the river about 15 miles. We carried a canoe about 6 miles through the woods from Mole Harbor to one lake and went through 2 lakes to the big one and down the river to the other side of the Island at Killisnoo. Well I hope I will hear from you soon. Enclosed find M.O. [money order] for $25. I will send some more when I get all my pay.[20]

Allen Hasselborg with bear shot at Rodman Bay, Baranof Island,
August 25, 1907. *Courtesy of Alaska Historical Library*

Back in Juneau two months later, he told his mother that it
had rained so hard most of the time, he had secured only two
more bears. The good news was that Miss Alexander wanted him
to hunt for her again next year.

> I am going to build a gasoline launch 25 ft.
> long with a cabin on it. I dont know how much it
> will cost so am only sending you $25. I would like
> to have Ira come up here if he wants to. Maybe I
> can make enough to send for him next summer.
> There was lots of work this year. He could make
> enough to get back if he dident want to stay. . . .
> There wont be any trouble about homesteads up

here. There is plenty of good land but very few homestead[s] taken. . . . I have got a little money in the bank too. But will have to spend it all for the launch I guess, but believe I can make money by having a launch.[21]

For Hasselborg, now thirty years old, the entire summer had been a dream come true. After eight years in Alaska, first drifting from job to job, then barely making ends meet on his own, he had been paid to do everything he liked doing and did well. He had spent almost three months with experienced naturalists who had taught him much about zoology and botany and who now promised to pay him for any specimens he could send them. And henceforth his name would appear twice, prominently, on maps of Admiralty Island.

6

BITTEN BY THE

PROUD BEAR

ALL THROUGH THE FALL of 1907, in a shed on Douglas Island, Hasselborg worked on his diesel launch. Though there were only a few other small motor boats in Alaska at the time and he had never built anything bigger than canoes and dories, he had a naval architect's plans he could modify to suit himself.

By February, the *Ebba* (named after his youngest sister) was in the water, waiting for her 7.6 horsepower engine to come up from Seattle. Twenty-five feet long, with an eight-foot cabin and a small forward berth, she would be his first real home in Alaska, a snug base for trapping in the winter and his ticket to hunt, fish, and prospect the rest of the year.

As spring approached, a flurry of letters came up from California. Annie Alexander reported that her 1907 expedition to southeastern Alaska had secured 1,008 bird and mammal specimens, including twenty-eight bears, twelve of which had been shot by Hasselborg. Her big news was that because of all the

Allen Hasselborg's launch *Ebba* under construction in shed at Lawson Creek, Douglas Island. *Courtesy of Alaska Historical Library*

new material from Alaska, she and Grinnell had founded a museum at the University of California in Berkeley.[1] Grinnell was now more eager than ever for bird specimens from Alaska, and Merriam was "wild"[2] to get hold of more bears, she said, especially *Ursus dalli*, a brown bear he was "all in a muddle about," and a rare, light-colored species he called a "glacier bear."[3] She wondered if Hasselborg would be interested in hunting at Yakutat, several hundred miles up the coast from Juneau, then joining her, Dixon, and several other naturalists for a summer of collecting in Prince William Sound. She would pay him $60 a month and $220 for camping gear and food and would also buy him a new rifle and all the ammunition he might need.[4]

Hasselborg readily accepted Alexander's offer. It would mean postponing his first summer excursion in the *Ebba*, but he would be paid to hunt bears again, besides getting a new rifle and the chance to explore a different part of Alaska. "I am very glad indeed that you are willing to go after bears for me this coming spring," Alexander wrote after receiving his reply. "I hope you have succeeded in getting the high powered .45/70 you wrote for. One needs a cannon to tackle those old giants with."[5]

Letters written by the Californians portray Hasselborg as a thin-skinned, though promising, rookie on the new museum's collecting team. "Hasselborg is just like a snake in the grass when it comes to sneaking up on things. He is honest and accurate in his observations," Dixon remarked to Grinnell at one point. "He doesn't know much about putting up skins and is rather impatient, but a little tact will smooth out the last and practice will overcome the first difficulty."[6] Alexander and Grinnell were

Juneau, December 1908. Allen Hasselborg's launch, the *Ebba* is in left foreground. *Courtesy of Alaska Historical Library*

Allen Hasselborg aboard *Ebba,* 1909. Self-portrait. *Courtesy of Alaska Historical Library*

always very polite to him and never too demanding, often following their requests to him with compliments and self-conscious appeals for advice. Having founded a museum they hoped would soon have the best collection of Alaska material in the country, they couldn't afford to offend the guide who had shown them so much of southeastern Alaska, the hunter who had saved Alexander from the embarrassment of returning to San Francisco with only a few bear specimens to show for her efforts.

After sending Hasselborg a box with everything he needed to prepare and label specimens, Alexander told Grinnell that she hoped her gift would encourage Hasselborg to "do some of the finer work."[7] Grinnell replied that while he was sure Hasselborg could learn to prepare better specimens, he was concerned that the Alaskan's devotion to bear hunting might distract him from collecting birds. Dixon, always the diplomat, reassured Grinnell that while Hasselborg felt as strongly about bears as Grinnell did about ptarmigan, he was confident that Hasselborg would be willing to shoot a few ptarmigan, especially if Alexander asked him to. Grinnell agreed with Dixon's suggestion that Hasselborg carry a revolver at all times, which might rid him of his distressing habit of collecting small birds with his .45/70; in a scientific report on the 1907 expedition, Grinnell had been forced to admit that the "fragments" of a particularly valuable bird specimen shot by Hasselborg had not been preserved.[8]

Although concerned about Hasselborg's performance as a collector, they respected his knowledge of wildlife and often included him in their scientific discussions. One of their favorite topics was Merriam's study of North American bears. Merriam was a "splitter," as taxonomists keen to proclaim new species on the basis of relatively few physical characteristics were—and are—called by their colleagues. With bears, for example, he relied heavily on measurements of their skulls and claws. Joseph Grinnell, on the other hand, belonged to a growing school of younger zoologists who doubted the value of such superficial work and were beginning to focus more on animal behavior and population distribution. Grinnell was skeptical of Merriam's conclusions about the bears Alexander brought back from Alaska. As a founder of a small new museum on the West Coast, however, he was not about to openly criticize the politically powerful director of the U.S. Biological Survey. Alexander, a former Merriam protégé who still depended on him to legitimize her bear collecting, followed Grinnell's lead.

Hasselborg certainly knew enough about bears by then to share their skepticism of Merriam. He also knew that Alaskan collectors selling to scientists from below often fudged information about specimens so they could sell more. Yet nowhere in his letters or journals from those early years is there any sign that he strongly objected to Merriam's research or regretted killing so many bears for science. Perhaps he hadn't yet formed a strong opinion on the subject; certainly he didn't want to risk losing such a steady source of income. When he found areas where hunters had greatly reduced the number of bears, he was frustrated only that others had gotten to them before him.

He also didn't seem to mind collecting many other kinds of mammals and birds, except when they kept him from hunting bears. While the painstaking work of skinning and labeling small specimens often annoyed him, his occasional prickliness with the Californians and Merriam went deeper than any frustration with the demands of scientific field work. Clearly he was unsettled by them. They came from a world of wealth and privilege he had never known—"the millionaire class," he called it[9]—and he was insulted when they seemed condescending or didn't give him credit for the work he'd done.

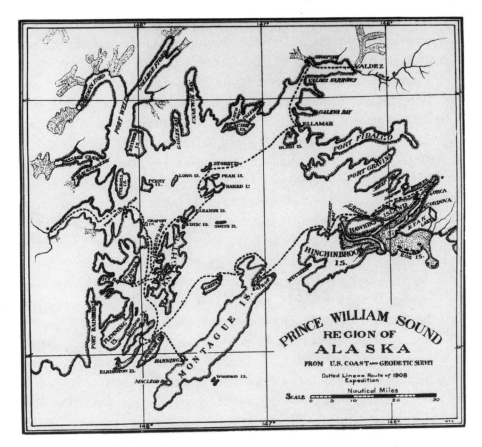

Map of the region traveled by the 1908 Alexander Alaska Expedition.
The dotted line shows the route of the expedition.
Courtesy of Alaska Historical Library

Yet despite his minor resentments and class-conscious insecurities, he respected and admired all of them. His dealings with Grinnell and Merriam, neither of whom he had met, were always reserved and businesslike. He was slightly warmer and more cordial to Alexander, a tough, independent lady who loved to hunt as much as he did. "I wish you could see Miss Alexander, the lady I have been working for," he wrote Flora. "You would be surprised to see her after she has been sleeping out under a tree for a week and helping to skin a few bears and cooking for the crowd."[10] A wry, left-handed tribute—credit to her for not being as dainty and snobbish as other upper class ladies he'd met—it was a compliment nonetheless, coming from someone who rarely expressed admiration for anyone. He had special affection for the affable, easy-going Joe Dixon, who was like a doting younger brother. The two young men had often hunted together during the summer of 1907 and had become fast friends. Now, as the date of their departure for Prince William Sound approached, they wrote each other regularly, with much discussion about guns, ammunition, and all the bears they planned to shoot.

Hasselborg arrived in Yakutat by steamer on April 1, 1908, with a canoe, a canvas tent, several blankets, a cook stove, pots and pans, a camera, various sizes of leg-hold traps, his .45/70 Winchester, a .38 revolver, and a 12-gauge shotgun Alexander had sent him. At the local store he spent $27.85 on groceries, enough to last several weeks. About four feet of snow was still on the ground, so he bought a sled, and, after hiring a local man to help him drag it, headed south down the railroad tracks out of town. At the mouth of the Ahrnklin River, he parted ways with his helper and set off upstream alone.

During the next two months, he also explored the Situk and Dangerous rivers, hauling and poling his canoe upstream, drifting back down with the current, hunting from two different base

Allen Hasselborg's camp, near Yakutat, 1908. *Photograph by A. Hasselborg.*
Courtesy of Alaska Historical Library

camps, through thickets of alder and willow and out across miles
of tide flats and rolling sandhills behind the beach. Away from
camp he slept under his canoe or at the base of a tree, wrapped in
blankets. He set traps for wolves and muskrat and collected
everything from northern pike spawning in the sloughs to a water ouzel nest with all its eggs. Despite relentless, driving rain,
high winds and freezing temperatures, he was able to shoot a river
otter, a fox, and a lynx.[11]

At Grinnell's request, he took detailed notes on the weather,
his travel route, and wildlife observations. "Shot strange bird and
skinned it . . . size hermit thrush," reads a typical entry in his

journal. "Brown mottled. Blue head, black crown with green spot in front and blue one behind."[12] "Fox den with young, 12 dead sparrows in front," reads another. "Bears have been trying to dig out fox cubs."[13] Along the river banks he found holes in the snow where bears had been digging out salmon carcasses from the previous summer. Although black bears were quite plentiful, he hunted more than a month before he shot and wounded one. While tracking it, he came upon a glacier bear standing in the wounded bear's tracks and easily killed it with two shots.[14] It was a female about four feet long from nose to tail, creamy white on both flanks, with a dark gray stripe down her back, a chocolate brown muzzle and a bluish-gray head. "Indians have no specific name for them, except 'Seegnoon' which means old, grey black bear," he wrote in his journal.[15] One of them had recently killed a light-colored bear cub traveling with two black bear cubs. "They were of the same family," he noted,[16] confirming what the Tlingits already knew: glacier bears were no more than a rare local color phase of the black bear.

When Alexander, Dixon, and two other naturalists arrived in Yakutat June 1, they were disappointed to learn that Hasselborg was still out hunting, though they were delighted with the glacier bear specimen and two brown bear cubs he had captured after shooting their mother. Before leaving for Prince William Sound, Alexander arranged for the cubs to be shipped down to the Golden Gate Park Zoo in San Francisco and wrote a note to Hasselborg commending him for having captured them.[17]

Hasselborg caught up with Alexander and her party three weeks later in Prince William Sound.[18] During the next three months, they collected specimens on fourteen islands and at five locations on the mainland. Besides bear hunting and his other collecting duties, Hasselborg ably skippered Alexander's thirty-two-foot sailboat, at one point rigging a new set of sails to cope

Allen Hasselborg feeding brown bear cubs, Yakutat, 1908. Pelt of cubs'
mother and a glacier bear (right) hang above his canoe. Note string
extending from his right hand to camera for self-portrait.
Courtesy of T. Davis

with the sound's erratic winds.[19] On almost every island he found
old bear trails and faded scratch marks on trees but very few bears,
sure signs that other hunters had been there before him. Nevertheless, he was able to shoot a few more, one of which came up
behind him as he was setting a trap. Another took six shots in the
chest before dying; it kept staggering around looking for him,
and his rifle got so hot he had to stop shooting for a while to let it
cool down.[20]

By September, Alexander and the others had returned to
California with more than a thousand specimens. Hasselborg went
back to Yakutat to try for more bears but managed to collect only
one black bear after almost a month of hunting. Late in October,

he marked the end of summer with a terse entry in his journal: "hard freezing ¾ in. ice."[21]

That winter, he lived aboard the *Ebba* at a wharf on Douglas Island. By February, he was complaining to his family that he had been laying in rough water all the time. It was "the coldest winter ever known" in Alaska, he said. The temperature had hovered around zero since Christmas, with "a gale of wind" that was constant. All the bays were frozen over and no one dared venture out of Gastineau Channel; already two men had been blown off the wharves and drowned.[22]

As spring approached, Grinnell wrote to ask him to collect on the islands south of Juneau, promising $125 a month to cover all

Allen Hasselborg at the helm of Anne Alexander's boat during 1908 Alexander Alaska Expedition to Prince William Sound. *Courtesy of University of California Museum of Vertebrate Zoology*

May. June.
Dall Island. Rocky Bays.

31st. Black Bear ♂ 5 ft 9 in. — 10½ in tail.
This bear started for me at the
first shot and was within 30 ft
when the third bullet hit it. the
first black bear I ever knew to show
fight. its lower jaw had been
broke probably fighting with another
bear.

June 3 Water dog in alchohol ♯ 16
June 3 Horn bill Aukles. ♯ 17
Saw a great deal of wolf sign
at Rocky Bay deep trails crossing
certain parks in every direction also
considerable bear sign. could have
done some trapping if time was not
limited. lots of deer also.

at. two bays south of cape August
very rocky and barren country. lots
of deer and wolf sign. too much
sea to land on Forrester Island.
Duke Island. saw no signs of any
large game except deer. saw lots
of deer and tracks of doe and young fawn

A page from Allen Hasselborg's hunting journal, 1909.
Courtesy of Alaska Historical Library

Black bear shot by Allen Hasselborg at Rocky Bay, Dall Island, described in his 1909 hunting journal, preceding page. *Courtesy of Sheppard family*

his expenses. Harry Swarth, a young naturalist recently hired by the museum, would be coming up to join him, Grinnell said. Concerned that Hasselborg might balk at collecting with someone he didn't know, Grinnell went to great lengths to assure him that Swarth was a perfect gentleman, good-natured under trying circumstances, and industrious and conscientious to a fault.[23] Hasselborg and Swarth got on fine, as it turned out, traveling together on the *Ebba* for more than four months and a thousand miles. Writing his mother from Juneau the first week of September, Hasselborg enclosed a money order for $100 and said he was in town just a short while to ship specimens down to

California and get ready to go out again. "I have only got 10 bears this year as we have been after small stuff mostly," he reported.[24]

In a letter to Grinnell, Swarth had said Hasselborg was "grouchy" from hunting in so many places where most of the black bears had been hunted out.[25] As for brown bears, they hadn't seen one all summer, although Hasselborg found some tracks along the Taku River. While it had been a disappointing bear hunt, Hasselborg had been able to explore much of the lower half of southeast Alaska, and the *Ebba* had performed well on her first long-distance cruise. They had also confirmed for Merriam that no coastal brown bears lived on the islands south of Baranof and had collected ten common yellowthroats, a songbird species previously known to breed only on the eastern slope of the Coast Mountains.

Back on Douglas Island that fall, Hasselborg sent Grinnell everything from loons and woodpeckers to a great horned owl someone had killed as it tried to fly off with a neighbor's cat. While collecting on Admiralty Island, he beached the *Ebba* at the mouth of a river on Seymour Canal before realizing he had come in at high water on a big tide. First gale-force winds came howling down the river valley, followed by eighteen inches of snow; then it poured rain for several days before he managed to float free and return to town. Still determined to collect some marten specimens Grinnell had requested, he was back on Admiralty by Christmas. It snowed a total of forty days in January and February, and he gave up after losing too many traps.

A year later, after trying to trap on Admiralty again, he sounded fed up with the winters in southeast Alaska:

> I got your letter and the scarf over a month ago
> but have been too disgusted with the weather to

Ebba iced in at Pleasant Bay, Admiralty Island, Christmas, 1910.
Note marten and mink on mast and foredeck.
Photograph by A. Hasselborg. Courtesy of E. Gardner

write or do anything else since. The climate seems to be getting worse up here every year for several years past. The scarf has been just the thing for this weather. It has been below zero with an awfull wind blowing most of the time. I am sending you a picture of my Christmas camp. I couldent get away from that place for two weeks and came near losing the boat when the ice closed in once. The winter came in so sudden that I dident have a chance to get any bear, and there is hardly any of the small fur animals left. I wish you could see this town now. They are shoveling snow off of the roofs and wharfs to keep them from breaking down.[26]

By the time spring arrived, his mood had improved. Merriam had written with an urgent request for the skins and skulls of any bears he could get, "regardless of sex, age, or species." In addition to a monthly salary of $150, Merriam was offering to pay him a dollar for black bear skulls and five dollars for brown bear skulls.[27] Hasselborg hadn't done much bear hunting since his disappointing summer with Swarth, so he was happy to go back to it full time. He went up the coast as far as Glacier Bay and south as far as Prince of Wales Island but ended up hunting mostly on the mainland near Juneau. At Montana Creek, about twenty miles north of town, the bears seemed to know he was after them. "Saw considerable sign but the bear are very wary," he wrote in his journal. "[They] stay in the brushyest and roughest places and only come out to fish at night."[28] Farther north, at Berners Bay, he shot a female brown bear and her two yearling cubs, then skinned and dissected them. Their stomachs were full of wild parsnip and meadow grass. The sow's udders were swollen with milk and the yearlings were too old to be nursing, so he guessed they were from a previous litter and had killed her younger cubs.

By September, he had collected six brown bears and four black bears. Two months later he wrote Flora to say that he was still trying for the brown bear skin she had asked for. Merriam had recently offered him $150 apiece for specimens of the right kind of bear, he said, so he was going out again, though it was late in the season and most of the bears had already denned up.[29]

When he wrote Flora again it was July 1912—eight months later. He hadn't killed a bear for her yet, he said, although he had seen several that spring: none had been worth shooting, as the spring had been very early and warm and they were already shedding. Things were booming in town, though. The year before, the Treadwell had showed its biggest profit ever, and now two of the other gold mines on Douglas Island were having record years of their own. The Alaska Gastineau Mine had just announced plans to construct a big hydroelectric dam at Salmon Creek and a new ore mill south of town. There were even some automobiles now, he said, six or seven of them, and it was dangerous to walk the streets.[30] Not that he spent any more time in town than he had to—just enough to ship his specimens, pick up his mail and resupply; town wasn't good for much else. He was on a boom of his own. Merriam had offered to continue his salary through the fall, and that spring he had guided a wealthy sportsman who promised to recommend him to other hunters. By now he had shot and trapped so many bears that they were just skins and skulls, money in his pocket. He had it down to a routine. Maybe that's why he got careless, why he would long remember the name of the Tlingit man he met in Glacier Bay a few weeks later.

He was hunting up the Bartlett River, looking for a big bear he'd tracked the summer before, when he encountered a party of Tlingit hunters.[31] While talking with them, he boasted that he wasn't afraid of bears. To the Tlingits, that was dangerous behavior. An older hunter named Albert Jackson sharply warned him that if he kept talking like that, a bear would get angry and attack him.

It may have been the next evening when he saw a large bear and fired four shots at it. The bear ran off with Hasselborg in hot pursuit. "Well, you know how bears hide and wait for you," he would say later. "That's what this one did; I was in a hurry because of the dark, and the first thing I knew, up jumped the bear from behind a ledge and started for me." He had time for only one desperate shot before the bear gathered him in and buried its teeth in his right elbow. Luckily, the sleeve of his jacket tore off in the bear's mouth and he was able to drop to the ground and lie motionless, face down in the mud, still clutching his rifle.

He knew playing dead was his only chance; just that spring a Juneau man caught by a bear had tried several times to escape, and each time the bear had returned to attack him.

After a while he cautiously stood up. He had no feeling in his arm; the bear's teeth had pulled a tendon several inches out and ripped loose a chunk of flesh. In the gathering darkness, he found his way back to the river and launched his skiff. He tried rowing with his left arm, three pulls to one side, three to the other, then tied an oar to the stern and sculled. Soon it was too dark to see, so he let the boat drift, blindly lurching and bumping down through several rapids, ten miles out to the bay. About midnight, he arrived back at the Tlingit hunters' cabin. He told them he needed help pulling the *Ebba's* anchors, as he couldn't do it with one arm, and that he also could use some help getting back to Juneau. One of them reluctantly agreed to go along. Albert Jackson, the old man, woke up long enough to say that Hasselborg had got what he deserved.

Back on the *Ebba*, Hasselborg's assistant hauled in her two anchors, then proceeded to run her up on some rocks. The tide was going out, so they were stuck for the next twelve hours. By the time she floated off, Hasselborg was sure he was going to lose the use of his arm. Eighty-five miles and half a day later, at two in the morning, he pounded on a Juneau doctor's front door. When nobody answered, he looked up another doctor, who woke up long enough to bandage his arm temporarily and suggest that he go to the hospital when it opened at nine. The hospital doctor was out on a maternity case, so Hasselborg walked all the way back to the first doctor, who cut out the ripped tendon and saved his arm. It had been two and a half days since the mauling and three days since he'd last slept.

His sister Flora must have been alarmed when she saw his letter with her address almost illegible on the envelope, and then

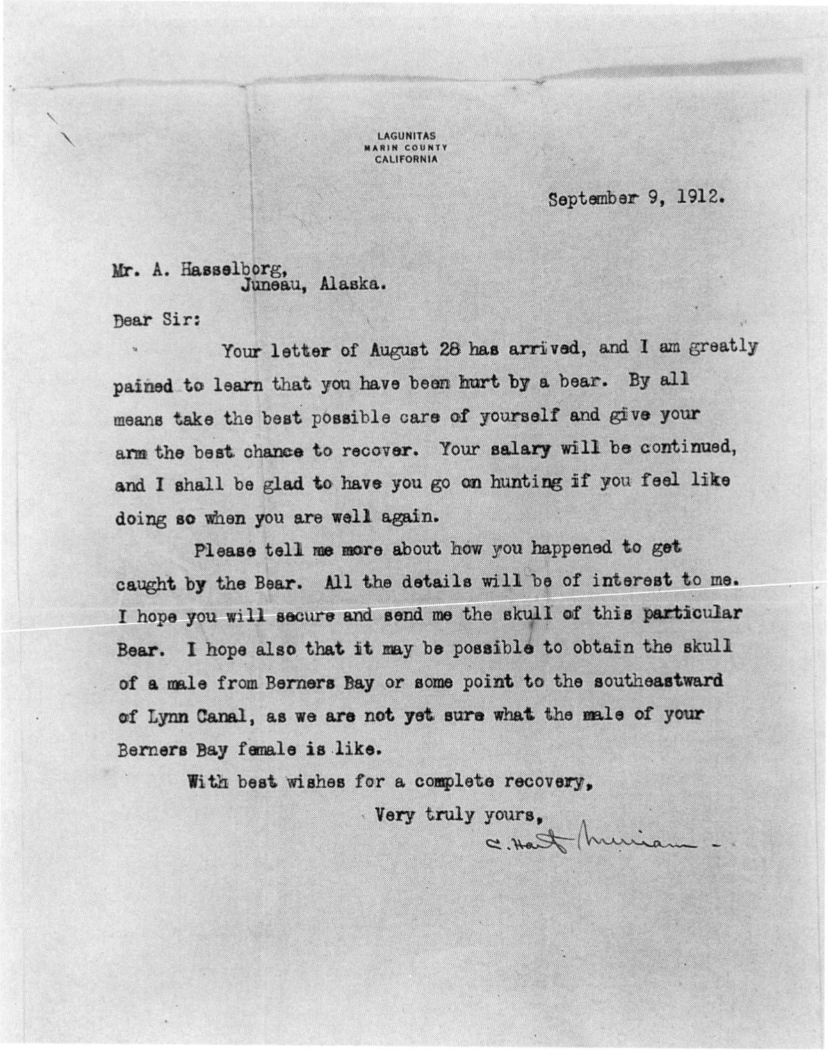

LAGUNITAS
MARIN COUNTY
CALIFORNIA

September 9, 1912.

Mr. A. Hasselborg,
      Juneau, Alaska.

Dear Sir:

     Your letter of August 28 has arrived, and I am greatly
pained to learn that you have been hurt by a bear. By all
means take the best possible care of yourself and give your
arm the best chance to recover. Your salary will be continued,
and I shall be glad to have you go on hunting if you feel like
doing so when you are well again.

     Please tell me more about how you happened to get
caught by the Bear. All the details will be of interest to me.
I hope you will secure and send me the skull of this particular
Bear. I hope also that it may be possible to obtain the skull
of a male from Berners Bay or some point to the southeastward
of Lynn Canal, as we are not yet sure what the male of your
Berners Bay female is like.

     With best wishes for a complete recovery,

          Very truly yours,

           C. Hart Merriam

Letter to Allen Hasselborg from C. H. Merriam after Glacier Bay mauling,
1912. *Courtesy of Alaska Historical Library*

his news inside, written in the same painfully clumsy hand. Writing with his left hand was hard work, he said. "A grizzlie started to eat me up but thought I was too tough so I got off with a bad right arm. I will be laid up for about a month more and believe the arm will be as good as ever."[32]

The naturalists at the museum in Berkeley soon learned of the attack and sent their condolences, congratulating him for eluding what Dixon called "that man-eating bear."[33] Merriam wrote to say that he was "greatly pained" to learn that Hasselborg had been attacked.[34] He was eager to hear the whole story and especially wanted the skull of that particular bear. "By all means take the best possible care of yourself and give your arm the best possible chance to recover. Your salary will be continued, and I shall be glad to have you go on hunting if you feel like doing so when you are well again."[35]

By the middle of September, the doctor had said Hasselborg could go hunting again. "I got only one large wound and it will not be skinned over for some time yet," he told his family cheerfully.

> I am in hopes that I will not have a stiff right arm but cannot move it at the elbow yet. I have been asked to get the skull of the bear that bit me, if possible, and will start out tomorrow. He ought to be dead by now, as I had shot him near the heart once and 4 times in the neck, but dident care to follow him up when he went off and left me with my right arm helpless.[36]

Six weeks after the mauling, although his arm was still almost useless, he went back up the Bartlett River and found the remains of the bear a hundred and fifty yards from where it had jumped him. Ravens and other scavengers had fed on the carcass,

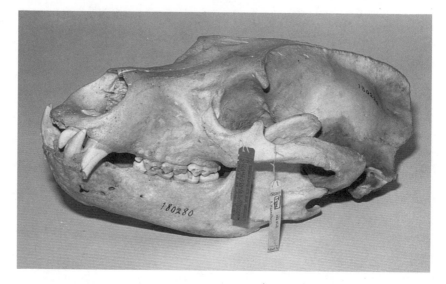

Skull of brown bear that mauled Allen Hasselborg. Type specimen of
Ursus orgilos. Collection of the National Museum of Natural History.
Photograph by J. Howe

scattering the bones, but he was able to find the skull and ship it
back to Merriam, who declared it the type specimen for a new
species: *Ursus orgilos*, the Proud Bear.[37]

Hasselborg was mostly just embarrassed by the whole affair.
He was reluctant to divulge many details to Merriam, and in a
letter to Swarth made a point of dismissing his crippled arm as a
minor annoyance.[38] It was his own fault, he said, getting caught
like that; he didn't blame the bear at all. At the same time, he was
proud he'd had the nerve to play dead when the bear jumped
him. In years to come, when he told the story of Merriam's Proud
Bear, he showed off his bear bite, and when he filled out government forms he used the scar as his identifying mark. A friend he

showed it to more than thirty years later said it looked as if a heavy spike had been driven into the muscle, then ripped out sideways.[39]

But he must have been more shaken up than he let on: coming around that rock outcrop and the bear suddenly right there, furious with pain, as wide as a horse, and towering over him. He must have thought, if only for an instant, that death was upon him, not just a bear. Certainly it was more than a coincidence that a few months after the mauling he told his family that although Merriam had asked him to start hunting again, he guessed he wasn't going to, not for a while anyway.[40] By the end of the next year he had built a small house, with a shop and three rooms, on Douglas Island, across from Juneau. At the age of thirty-six, for the first time since arriving in Alaska, he had it "a little comfortable," he said, in a home of his own.[41] He had decided to settle down.

7

TOO MANY

NEIGHBORS

FROM HIS HOUSE on Douglas Island, Hasselborg could look straight across Gastineau Channel at Juneau. While Juneau hadn't grown much since he'd first seen it, it was now a more respectable cluster of neat clapboard houses, hotels, and apartment buildings dominated by a stately new courthouse on Telephone Hill. Along the waterfront, where at the turn of the century skiffs had lined a rocky beach, a jumble of wharves and commercial warehouses now spilled out over the channel. Three miles south down the beach were the adjoining towns of Douglas and Treadwell, which, due to the continued success of the Treadwell Mines, had a population of about three thousand, twice that of Juneau.

All three were hard-working mining towns whose fortunes rose and fell with the price of gold and the engineers' latest schemes, company towns where the mine owners came and went like royalty and the pounding of the ore mills reverberated off the mountains day and night. They were frontier towns where

House built by Allen Hasselborg on Douglas Island, 1913. Gastineau Channel and Juneau in background. *Photograph by A. Hasselborg. Courtesy of T. Davis*

payday was announced in advance so local merchants and saloonkeepers could prepare for the miners' arrival downtown; bawdy, rough towns where ladies of the night did a brisk business along South Franklin Street; complacently bigoted towns where the original inhabitants of the area, the Tlingits of the Auk tribe, had been reduced to an underclass unable to vote and banned from many local establishments.

They were gossipy, small communities where the telephone operator knew most people's two-digit numbers and reports of boys shooting out streetlights with slingshots, the results of bowling competitions, and news of the mayor's latest bear hunt made the front page of the paper. They were lively, fun-loving towns, constant rivals that competed at almost any sport at the drop of a hat. Several large theaters offered vaudeville, plays, and musicals performed by troupes from "below," as locals then called the rest of the United States. Raucous smokers at the Elks Hall and the Treadwell Club featured prize fights and wrestling matches. Orchestras and bands of every size and description played at dances, accompanied picture shows, serenaded swimming competitions at the Treadwell Club, and entertained roller skaters at Jaxon's Rink on the Juneau waterfront. And yet though they were bustling, thriving communities with more people than any other towns in Alaska, they were still just pinpricks on the map, a faint hum of human activity isolated by wilderness stretching for thousands of miles in every direction. Seattle was four days and nights away by steamship, no road connected them to the outside world, and it would be a few more years before the first airplane flew down Gastineau Channel.

In 1913, the year Hasselborg built his house, so many new buildings were going up that Juneau's main sawmill was expanding to meet the demand. The mining companies were continuing to invest millions in the Alaska-Juneau and Alaska-Gastineau mines, construction of the big Salmon Creek hydroelectric project was well under way, and a new cold storage facility for the fishing fleet had just opened for business on South Franklin Street. Juneau was all abuzz over the first territorial legislature, which after much discussion had decided to convene at the Elks Hall.

Writing his mother, Hasselborg dismissed Alaska's first legislators as "good corporation men."[1] Like many Alaskans, he resented the monopolization of the territory's resources by large outside companies and suspected the government of colluding with them. Most irksome was the corporations' opposition to home rule. Fearing higher taxes if the territory was given more control of its own affairs, they and their allies in Congress had sought to perpetuate the popular image of Alaska as an empty icebox with a population too small and transient to govern such a vast area.

During the early 1900s, trust busters, conservationists, and other reformers led by President Theodore Roosevelt had partially frustrated the corporations and their conservative allies by putting some of Alaska's more valuable resources outside their grasp. "For the conservatives Alaska was a region of great potentialities whose development was being thwarted by addlepated reformers," as Ernest Gruening explains in *The State of Alaska*.

> For the reformers Alaska was likewise a great frontier of potential settlement which must be rescued from the tentacles of the corporate octopus. . . . Both schools of thought had their supporters in Alaska. This conflict was to underlie Alaskan politics and economics for the next half century. Alaska would become a battleground between the contending forces, and its people the victims of clashing theory and practice.[2]

Clear evidence of the impact of that conflict had come with the 1910 U.S. census. While the population of the rest of the country had grown by twenty-one percent during the first decade of the century, with every state and two territories showing marked increases, Alaska had grown only by about one percent. Whether reformers blaming large outside corporations or conservatives blaming "addlepated reformers" in Washington, D.C., many Alaskans felt victimized by distant political forces limiting economic development of the territory.

At times that xenophobia had taken particularly nasty turns, as in 1906 when James Wickersham, a leading candidate for Alaska's nonvoting seat in Congress, successfully exploited an undercurrent of anti-Semitism by attacking "the Guggenheims," part owners of one of the more powerful outside companies operating in the territory.[3]

During the first decade of the century, conflicts between conservatives and trust-busting reformers had also occurred at the national level. In 1910, they erupted within the Republican administration of President William Taft when Gifford Pinchot, the head of the U.S. Forest Service, openly accused Secretary of the Interior Richard Ballinger of favoring certain corporate interests trying to exploit valuable tracts of Alaskan coal lands. Taft fired Pinchot, which caused a major rift in the Republican Party and led to the founding of the Progressive Party the following year. In the 1912 presidential election, Theodore Roosevelt, the Bull Moose or Progressive candidate, and Taft, a conservative stand pat Republican, both lost to Woodrow Wilson, a Democrat.

In the letter to his mother in which he sneered at the "good corporation men" in the legislature, Hasselborg said he was sure he wasn't a stand pat Republican and believed he was a Progressive.[4] As a laborer working for a dollar a day at an Arizona copper mine, as a fisherman who returned from his first trip to Alaska poorer than when he left, as a miner wracked by rheumatism after months of "terrible hard work" in the Treadwell mines, he had seen plenty of America's business from the bottom looking up.[5] He thought of himself as a working man a world apart from the millionaire owners of the big corporations and the conservative Republicans who looked after their interests. As for voting for a Democrat, that was clearly not a possibility, and certainly not a suitable topic for discussion in a letter to his staunch Republican mother.

And yet, on election day in August 1912, he had been a hundred miles from town, headed for Glacier Bay and his fateful encounter with Merriam's Proud Bear, and he said he only *believed* he was a Progressive. Cynical about politics since his teens, when he argued with his mother about the Spanish-American War, he didn't seem to care much which party he supported or even whether he voted at all.[6] "I wish you wouldn't worry so much about politics," he chided his mother in 1914. "I think the worse things get, the better it will be. So what's the use of worrying."[7]

It was a misanthrope's view of the world—narrow-minded, occasionally bigoted. He had a typical Alaskan's resentment of outsiders, some of it justified, some of it liable to slip into the facile anti-Semitism Wickersham had exploited. He was quick to blame "Hebrew fur smugglers," for example, whenever fur prices dropped too low.[8] Frustrated by Alaska's often vague and erratic game regulations and annoyed by its restrictive land laws, he would be even quicker to blame his troubles on politicians—all politicians. "There is a surplus of politicians," he told his mother. "I never vote and go around with a chip on each shoulder and bawl out every politician I meet. They take the other side of the street."[9] In the years ahead those chips would only get heavier as he increasingly channeled his frustrations into feuds with the Forest Service, the Game Commission, and any other government officials who tried to tell him what to do.

His feistiness—the fierce self-reliance of an American proud to be descended from a Revolutionary War hero, a Mohawk Indian, and an arrogant and impenitent Vermont preacher—was at times admirable. His passionate resentment of authority, however, came from deeper inside him than any democratic ideals he may have learned or any wrongs, real or imagined, he may have suffered at the hands of the government: probably it came from his childhood, from the wounds left by his father. All his life it would fester just below the surface, often breaking out in fits of anger that left him ever more isolated and alone.

"I don't know if I could ever work in a crowd again," he would tell his family. "It has been 12 years since I had to take orders from anyone. I am the boss even when I go out with the millionaires."[10] He planned to build and sell dories and guide wealthy sportsmen whenever he could. For that, he needed a new launch and had already worked out plans for a "cruiser" about the same length as the *Ebba*.[11] She would have the same size engine but be broader of beam and have a raised deck in front for more headroom in the cabin. No matter what, he wanted to avoid town as much as possible. Explaining to his family why he hadn't mailed a letter he had written the week before, he said he only got over to Juneau occasionally. "The fuss and hustle around town is enough to near drive me crazy, as I don't like towns."[12]

Though he lived a solitary bachelor life on the beach a safe distance from Douglas and the channel was a quarter-mile moat protecting him from Juneau, he was at least cordial to his neighbors. He would say later that during those years he had practically raised a boy who lived nearby, and that an old woman took such a shine to him she kept sneaking the socks off his clothesline and darning them until they were "mostly darn."[13] And it was in those years that he had what may have been his only even slightly flirtatious relationship with a woman. When he mentioned her years later, he said only that she was "a half breed" attending "Indian school" and that she wrote him on stationery with red borders like *Newsweek* magazine.[14] He didn't say whether he wrote her back, and his description of her as "a half breed" hardly denotes affection. Yet he said "the gals" at the post office teased him about her fancy stationery as if they sensed something was going on, at least for her. Whatever it was, it ended not long

Allen Hasselborg after cutting bow stem for *Bulldogg,* 1912. Self-portrait.
Courtesy of Alaska Historical Library

after it began. Many years later he would say that she married one of his friends and had fourteen children.[15] For the rest of his life, he would be no more than courteously acquainted with any woman outside his own family. As a boy, he had been painfully shy around girls his own age; as a teenager in Florida, he had been sharply critical of his sisters' beaus and contemptuous of marriage. The only strong role model he'd had while growing up was his father's rude indifference to his mother. Several years after his possible brief flirtation, he would say to a friend that all married men are "weak in the knees."[16] Probably he never decided not to get married, he was just too set in his ways and couldn't imagine letting anyone in so close.

In the spring of 1913, he guided an English sportsman on a bear hunt and took an engineer out on a two-week survey of potential hydropower sites near Juneau.[17] By that fall, however, he was having what he described as "a lot of little troubles."[18] First, the shortage of lumber in town forced him to delay work on his new launch. Then a man who had promised to buy the *Ebba* backed out, and he had to sell her for almost nothing. Writing his mother, he said it would take all the money he had to see him through until spring.[19]

It didn't help that right about then two of the biggest mines in town ran into trouble. A low gold price, increased shipping costs, and a labor shortage caused by America's imminent entry into the war in Europe were already hurting the mines when the Alaska-Gastineau unexpectedly hit low-grade ore and the Alaska-Juneau's new mill failed its first tests. As Juneau's economy faltered again, Hasselborg had trouble selling his dories.[20] Then several sportsmen who had hired him as a guide canceled out at the last minute. At one point he was so desperate, he admitted to Swarth, he sold three bear skins illegally to a bureaucrat.[21]

In 1915, he finished his new launch, the *Bulldogg*,[22] and began to roam again: to the outer coast to collect seabirds for the museum in Berkeley and down to Kuiu Island, at the southern end of the panhandle, on a two hundred-mile round-trip to buy furs. By then Dr. Merriam was barraging him with requests for bear specimens, offering up to two dollars for black bears and between two and ten dollars for brown bears, depending on their size and the condition of the hides. "I want everything," he told Hasselborg, "cubs and females as well as old males, and would like both skins and skulls of all that you kill yourself."[23] Merriam especially wanted big bears from Admiralty Island, where he was sure there were still several species left to be named.

So once again Merriam's quest lured Hasselborg out of town, back to "The Brown Bear's Fort Island."[11] He was restless and eager to be off on his own; Douglas Island was getting too crowded, he said. "I have got my downstairs full of neighbors," he told his family in 1916, "and their [dog] 'Buster' is making a great racket. They are preparing to build near me. There is to be a bridge built across to Juneau next summer and then I will have too many neighbors I guess."[24] That spring, he prospected for minerals up at Hasselborg Lake; by that summer, he was living aboard the *Bulldogg* at Mole Harbor and clearing a site for a garden on the north side of Mole River.[25] During the winter of 1917, the temperature dropped as low as fifteen below zero, deep snow made trapping difficult, and he came into town in the spring with only fifteen mink for sale. Nevertheless, he was thinking about filing for a homestead at Mole Harbor.[26]

Even before he had camped there with Alexander and she named a lake and a river for him, he had been drawn to that part of Admiralty Island. Almost every year since 1904 he had fished and trapped along Seymour Canal; Mole Harbor felt like home. Seventy miles out of Juneau, with a line of reefs guarding its entrance, it was a separate place, a private world. Three species of salmon spawned in Mole River. In the bay were halibut, herring, crab, and shellfish. Seals and porpoises swam in with the tides, and from out in Seymour Canal came the huge, soft breathing of humpback whales and a sound like thunder when they breached and fell back on the water. Thousands of migrating ducks, geese, and shorebirds stopped by in the spring and fall. Deer were plentiful, and so were bears. When Hasselborg's mother asked about coming up to live in Alaska, he sent her glowing reports, though he warned her it was twenty-five miles to the nearest neighbor. "There won't be any trouble about vegetables," he assured her. "They do wonderful well here. And you can spear tons of salmon in the creek with a pitchfork and shoot deer and bear in the garden."[27]

If he had any doubts about moving out to Mole Harbor, a major disaster at the Treadwell mines made up his mind. Driven by steadily falling profits, ignoring warnings from a number of smaller cave-ins in recent years, the Treadwell Company decided to go after richer ore in sections of rock that supported the mine workings deep underground.[28] On April 21, 1917, millions of gallons of sea water burst through from Gastineau Channel. Entire buildings disappeared as the surface caved in, and three of the mines were completely destroyed. Miraculously, no miners were killed, though hundreds of people were suddenly out of work. By the end of the year, Douglas and Treadwell would be virtual ghost towns, and Juneau would be in one of the worst economic slumps in its thirty-seven-year history. "I thought you might still be wanting to come up here but you had better not," he wrote his mother in May 1917. "Things were bad before, the price of gold and wages staying down, but now the bay has fell thru into the treadwell mines and they are a total loss. 3,000 feet deep and full of water. The payroll was about $250,000 per month and was the main support of these towns. . . . A lot of people are going farming."[29]

Less than a month after the cave-in, Hasselborg sold his house on Douglas Island for only $150. "I had spent $450 and a lot of hard work on it," he said.[30] Before long, he was planting his first garden at Mole Harbor. By October, he had harvested a bumper crop of vegetables and was full of plans for the future. "I know I will have some good hunting parties as soon as the wars are over," he told Flora. "I wish you could come up to the northwest with your boys. It is the only country. I couldent live in a country that had no mountains or scenery or climate. Florida never had a climate and you don't know it. . . . You would be surprised at the number of southern people up here from Ga., Ala., ect."[31] He had even made some money recently, he said, guiding two millionaires from Cleveland who had come up with a cameraman to take moving pictures of Alaskan wildlife.[32] In a few weeks, they had shot over five thousand feet of film, including some scenes of bears that the cameraman said were as "exciting as the devil."[33]

By fall, he had settled into a small cabin he built back behind the first bend in Mole River, right where a trapper had lived in the 1890s until a bear killed him.[34] The winter of 1918 was worse than the one before it—much worse. It would set his standard for every bad winter to come. The first big storm hit early in November, and by the end of March, the snow was so deep he had given up trying to dig out the front door and had taken to climbing out an upstairs window to fetch wood and water. Writing Flora the next spring, he sounded frightened by five lonely months of cold and darkness. Snow had covered the downstairs window so he was really "in a cave" for several months, he said.[35] "Had lots of grub and wood but could not do anything not even trap as the snow was deep even in Dec[ember]," he told his mother. "Glad you was not up here, and don't think of coming. There is too much lost time here in the fall and winter, account of the weather. Am going to try to sell out and go below."[36]

Was he serious about leaving Alaska, or just trying to discourage his sixty-five-year-old mother from coming up to live with him? Soon after the Treadwell cave-in, he had told her that rents were cheap in Juneau; perhaps he now regretted it. Anyway, he didn't go below, and it would be several years before he mentioned that possibility again. Before long, the shock of that awful winter had softened into the lush beauty of an Alaska spring. He would spend the entire summer of 1918 gardening and felling trees, leaving his homestead occasionally to do some prospecting in the mountains but only going into town once. "We had a wonderful summer," he told his family happily as another fall came around. "Wish you could see the vegetables I have got."[37]

Late one night that October, in the middle of the first big snowstorm, he was awakened by something shaking the cabin. At first, he thought it was an earthquake, but then he heard glass breaking, so he got up and cautiously peered downstairs. A bear was trying to climb in through the window; its front paws were on the sill and its head was already inside when it suddenly drew back and disappeared. Hasselborg grabbed his rifle and rushed to the window. Even through falling snow, the moon was so bright he could see the bear standing about eighty yards away. Quickly he aimed and fired, and the bear became a still, dark mound wrapped in whiteness.[38]

For years afterwards, he made a point of saying that he shot his last bear that night.[39] It was only rubbing its back against his cabin, he said, that's what woke him up. There was so much wet snow plastered on the shingles that it couldn't smell what was

97

View from Glass Peninsula, Admiralty Island (at South Island). Mainland in background. *Photograph by J. Howe*

inside and got curious. He was sorry he had killed it, he said. When asked why he wasn't shooting bears any more, he explained that it was too much work curing the pelts and he couldn't get a decent price for them any more.[40] But did killing one so close to home have something to do with it? Did he realize that he couldn't keep shooting them without meeting the same fate as the trapper who lived there before him? "The reason [bears] are sometimes ugly is probably because someone had shot at them sometime before," he would say later to one of his nephews.[41] Certainly by then he was fed up with Merriam's quest. "This year will probably see the finish of the bears as the Indians and everybody are getting excited over Dr. Merriam's $40 bounty on bear skulls," he wrote Harry Swarth.[42] He was skeptical of Merriam's most recent scientific paper, which listed no less than eighty-six species of North American brown and grizzly bears. "I got Dr. Merriam's review of the brown bears and it has got me up a stump for sure," he told Swarth. "I am quite sure the data on some of his type specimens was faked. . . . I sent him two old bears from Admiralty that were neighbors and either brothers or cousins, and he called one a grizzly and the other a brown."[43]

He was through with Merriam and through with killing bears. He would keep guiding bear hunters to make money, but he wouldn't shoot any himself, and he would try to get along with those around his place. No one would be allowed to hunt them; Mole Harbor would be a sanctuary for bears.[44]

8

RANCHER

HASSELBORG HAD BIG PLANS when he first moved out to Mole Harbor. Besides living off his garden and the country, he hoped to raise goats and hogs and sell vegetables to fishermen and to grocers in town. To make what little cash he needed, he would trap during the winter and guide hunters and photographers the rest of the year. He was really on his own now. Inside the back cover of one of his journals, in the space provided next to "In Case of Accident Notify," he wrote "Nobody."[1]

More pressing than any other task, however, was the legal requirement that he secure a patent to his homestead. After formally applying for 135 acres, he had only a few years to show that he had been improving them. Like many of Alaska's land laws, the homesteading law had been adapted from similar statutes in the states. It required him to clear the forest at a rate geared to the relatively gentle topography and sparse vegetation of the western plains, not the heavily forested coast of southeastern Alaska.[2] He had to work "like a mule," he said, to prove up on his place.[3]

Most of the trees were big spruce and hemlock, about a hundred per acre.[4] With only an ax and a cross-cut saw, he first had to clear out rotting logs tumbled together on the ground like giant match sticks, some more than a hundred feet long and four feet in diameter, many with young saplings growing out of them in gnarly tangles of trunks and branches. Then came days of felling standing trees, and more days sawing and chopping to limb them and cut what he needed for firewood. As for the stumps, his experience as a "bulldozer" in the Treadwell mines served him well. In one letter to Flora, he said he hadn't built any fences yet, as he'd been "blasting big stumps which fly several hundred yards."[5] Even when the stumps were out, there were still big piles of branches to burn, often a frustrating task because it rained so much. In the wettest weather, he said, his clearing was nothing but "mud and muck."[6]

In 1919, the year he applied for his patent and two years after he moved to Mole Harbor, he guessed that at the rate he was going it would take about five hundred years to get the place nicely cleared.[7] Two years later, he dug eighty bushels of potatoes from a quarter acre and predicted he would have several more acres ready for planting the next spring. By 1923, he had used three hundred pounds of dynamite to clear a little less than two acres.[8] 1925: "I have got the worst two acres of my ranch grubbed clear in 8 years, so you can figure out how long it will take to clear 135 acres."[9] 1926: "Will soon have enough land cleared to make a living on."[10] In 1928, he proudly reported that ten acres were partly ready for planting, that he had "destroyed" about five hundred trees,[11] and that people in Juneau were saying he was "a hero or a fool" for all the work he'd done.[12]

By then, his ambitious plans to raise goats and hogs and sell vegetables were long forgotten. Besides his main tasks of tending the garden, clearing trees, and running his traplines during the

Allen Hasselborg's cabin, Mole Harbor, 1930s or early 1940s.
Courtesy of F. Hibben

winter, he always had more work to do maintaining his cabin and boats, preserving and storing food, curing furs, sharpening and fixing tools, and all the daily chores of fetching water, chopping and hauling firewood, cooking, cleaning, washing, and mending. He was now in his early fifties, and though according to one friend he was as strong as an ox, he was beginning to feel his age. His rheumatism often bothered him and his teeth were giving him trouble. "I have been to the Dentist and had my teeth X rayed," he told his family at one point. "Two good teeth were ulcerated and had to be pulled and there was an old pus pocket that has been poisoning me for over 20 years. The dentist said I had been a neurotic for a long time on account of it."[13]

As the practical realities of homesteading sank in, his ambitions became smaller and simpler. "I am getting rather funny," he told Joseph Dixon in 1929. "I enjoy grubbing and chopping most of anything it seems."[14] He had given away his phonograph, had taken only one photograph in the last two years, and had yet to use the new movie camera a friend had given him. He owned a radio, and he tuned in the news now and then, but it was all about the foolish world outside, so he never listened long. More than ever now, he was ruled only by the weather and the changing seasons. "The only dates I ever notice are on the tide tables," he told Flora one year.[15]

From his letters to family and friends, from the reminiscences of those who knew him, and from several daily journals he left behind, it's possible to piece together the solitary, industrious life he led at Mole Harbor for the next twenty-four years. The journals, though few in number and often indecipherable, give the most intimate, coherent picture. Without fail, he recorded the date, temperature, weather, and a terse summary of each day's main event written phonetically and slurred into a single word— a private code. "[M]anyhumps" meant many humpback whales feeding in Seymour Canal; "sportstulaiks" reported sportsmen heading up to Lake Alexander; "baknbredalitlsno" described a day with a light snowfall spent baking bread; "krikfroz" announced the arrival of winter, "abar" (a bear) the coming of spring.[26]

The first bear usually appeared in late April or early May, hungrily nipping at the salty sedge grass in his tide meadow. By then, he already had most of his vegetables sprouting in boxes next to the cabin and was busy turning over the rich compost of seaweed, hay, and salmon he had spread over the garden the

Allen Hasselborg's garden at Mole Harbor (date unknown). Note on back of photo reads: "Cauliflower, ect. I had them much bigger other years."
Courtesy of P. Sheppard

previous fall. Most years, he planted lettuce, cabbage, beets, onions, potatoes, peas, spinach, turnips, carrots, and half a dozen other vegetables, along with perennial strawberries, raspberries, and an assortment of flowers.[17] The flowers were a casual experiment—mostly wild plants he brought in from the woods. "I have got foxgloves poppies ect. naturalized," he told Flora one year, "and let them fight it out with the weeds, and throw some other flower and vegetable seed around and let them do what they can."[18]

A page from Allen Hasselborg's weather journal, October 1947.
Courtesy of Alaska Historical Library

Gardening in southeastern Alaska required coping with an erratic climate and short growing season, besides maintaining a stout defense against hungry animals. The soil in Hasselborg's garden was two or three feet of rich black loam, so most years it did quite well. In his journals, he could get a little carried away describing it: "Weedsradishletucburnstumpsnoseeums" summed up a busy day weeding radishes and lettuce and burning stumps while fending off no-see-ums.[19] He might harvest a thousand pounds of potatoes, strawberries two inches across, and cabbages as big as water buckets. If it stayed wet and cold, though, his potatoes took on strange shapes, and his squash and cucumbers rotted; if it was too dry, he couldn't keep up with the watering. Some summers, almost everything went wrong. "My garden was near a total failure this year," he wrote Flora one fall. "It was first [too] wet and cold and then there was a 5 week drought and 80° weather and the deer have eaten the remains, all but the potatoes."[20]

Deer were often a nuisance, though a sturdy picket fence kept out all but the most determined raiders.[21] Bears were a problem, too, especially when they broke in and dug up potatoes or trampled the strawberries. Occasionally they rummaged through his wood shed or clawed up one of his skiffs. His dealings with them had to be delicate. "How can I give them a big fright without making them too peevish?" he asked Dixon one year.[22] For the most part, he got along with them. It was a matter of getting to know their individual peculiarities, learning their daily movements around the place, and staying out of their way.[23] Sometimes they just needed a good scolding. Karl Lane, a bear hunting guide, remembered landing at Mole Harbor and seeing Hasselborg standing in front of a huge sow with two cubs that had just crashed into his garden: "He was shaking his finger at them, but we couldn't hear what he was saying to them. The bears all stood there for a long time on their hind legs, but when they saw about ten of us coming along the beach, they took off and ran away."[24]

That was one service the bears provided—alerting him to the arrival of visitors. Along with ravens and eagles, they were his "watchdogs," he told one visitor, and he didn't have to feed them or clean up after them, he said.[25] He viewed the other wild animals at Mole Harbor with the same practical eye; if they weren't somehow useful to him, he didn't bother them and just tried to get along with them. While he saw himself as a "rancher," he was also the chief warden of a large, private game park with shifting boundaries.[26] He didn't allow hunting of any kind anywhere near his homestead, and for a number of years was also a stream guard, deputized by the Territorial Game Department, to keep fishermen from catching salmon too close to Mole River.[27]

Karl Lane was one of several Juneau people who encountered one of Hasselborg's more irregular regulations. After anchoring in Mole Harbor one spring day, Lane and another guide, Oscar Oberg, took several hunters around to Pleasant Bay, leaving behind a couple named Swanson. While Lane was gone, the Swansons visited Hasselborg and got permission for Mrs. Swanson to shoot one of his bears—or so they thought. When Lane returned, they told him about their conversation with Hasselborg, and although Lane was skeptical, he agreed to go in with them later the same day. "Hasselborg was really happy to see us, glad to see Oscar, who was an old friend," Lane remembered.

> He invited us in and out came that tin box full of pictures and we started looking at them, passing them around. Oscar and I—we just sat back there in the corner. I was smoking my pipe, talking quietly to Oscar a little bit. We figured we were going to let Swanson handle the whole situation.

Pretty soon it was getting dark. Finally Swanson said, Well, Mr. Hasselborg, it's true, isn't it, that you told Barbara that she can shoot one of your bears? And Hasselborg kind of glanced up a little bit and he said, Well, sure, Mr. Swanson. Now, Barbara might see one of my bears at Pleasant Bay, or she might see one of my bears at Gambier Bay, or she might see one at Pybus Bay, and she can shoot one of my bears there. But she can't shoot one of my bears here in Mole Harbor.[28]

"Swanson was madder than a wet hen," Lane recalled. "He never spoke a word. He got up, slapped his hat on his head, and he was the first one out the door."[29]

Hasselborg always talked about the animals at Mole Harbor as if he owned them. Besides being a rancher and a game warden, he was also the head keeper of an unruly menagerie. Visitors at various times reported a tame deer that liked having its nose rubbed, a gull acting at home in his front yard, a weasel popping into the cabin for hand-outs. He welcomed wild animals, watched over them, helped them when he felt like it.[30] In the peace and solitude of Mole Harbor, they kept him mindful of the seasons. They entertained and informed his inquiring, scientific mind. They were company.

His other, much less frequent company almost always came during the summer: tourists or members of his family visiting from the states, or people from Juneau. The tourists were definitely a mixed lot. Most had heard about him through friends and notified him in advance that they were coming; others dropped in unannounced on big boats, wearing fancy clothes and looking as if they had never set foot outdoors. He usually let them come ashore, though they tended to make themselves a bit too much at home, poking at things and asking too many questions.[31] Most didn't know how to act around his bears and scared them off. The worst of them spent most of their time on their yachts drinking and carrying on.

"Have been pretty busy and don't hardly know where I am at," he told Flora one summer.[32] His nephew, Raymond Sheppard, had visited and so had five yachts full of "the upper class" from Boston.[33] Raymond had received stern travel instructions from his Uncle Allen:

> Well it seems you really mean to visit me, so I am sending a money order to see that you don't get stuck. I don't think it would see you all the way by the Southern Pacific line and boats from S.F. The second class Seattle to Juneau is $26, probably less on the "Northland." I just got a telegram of Feb. 14, asking me to be the "wise guy" all season on a yacht. Cant learn yet whether this offer is still good so I dont know if I would be home if you came except at times. If I get the job there would be an old sourdough on the place and you could stop with him if you dident get a job of some kind. That Panama trip would be all right if you can make it, but your real trouble would be to get from Juneau to my place if I am away. If you start don't let anyone know you have money or where it is, as there is sure to be at least one thief in the crew of a ship. If you get to Seattle go to the Alaska Bureau of the Chamber of Commerce. Chas. Garfield who is in charge knows me, and could tell you of chances to get up the coast, and ask for Campbell Church's outfit, the one I may go with. . . . And be sure to look for my old friend

Louis Maag. Believe he still lives at 3962 Evanston
Ave Seattle. If you come let me know when you
might arrive. If I wasent there inquire at Truesdales
Gen. Store or Bloomgrens Grocery. And dont brag
about all the game you will kill as I am now a
deputy warden. . . . Dont get any clothes or shoes
ect. for the trip if you start, and if you dont come
use the money order the best way you can. Well I
hope we have a good visit but if I am away most of
the time you can probably get a job. Let me know
at once what the chances are of your coming, as I
am not in very often, and write two letters one to
Juneau and one to Gambier. If you are stuck in
Juneau go to the Government offices and ask for
a job. Forest Service, Fisheries, Survey Office,
Bureau of Roads, ect.[34]

Apparently the seventeen-year-old had ignored Hasselborg's
request for advance warning of his arrival date. "I was about tired
out when he arrived. Had made several trips to Juneau and
Gambier Bay to get news of him, 700 miles or more in all," he
groused to Flora.[35] Though he had enjoyed hunting and fishing
with the boy, he thought Raymond had showed just a little too
much initiative.

The next year, when another nephew, Allen Merritt, wrote
to ask if he could visit, too, Hasselborg made it clear that he
would not tolerate any more seven-hundred-mile mix-ups.
"You would have to arrive exactly on date and according to
schedule," he warned. "I wouldent be free and able to put in a
whole month running around looking for you as I did for
Raymond."[36] And this time he meant to curb any excessive
displays of boyish energy:

Now I don't know just what to do about you. Could you stick around the ranch by yourself at times for a short spell? You could botanize, fish, photograph, garden and amuse yourself otherwise, and when parties were around probably pick up some cash from them if you could backpack, cook, ect. How old are you and how big?[37]

Overnight visitors slept on the cabin floor and soon learned that there was nothing fancy about Hasselborg's cuisine. If left uneaten at breakfast, huge, half-cooked pancakes an inch thick and a foot across would be served again later in the day. A typical dinner was venison stew, trout or halibut, potatoes and fresh vegetables, and strawberries for dessert.[38] "Honest grub," he called it—food he hadn't bought in a store.[39] Guests who asked for anything he didn't have or didn't feel like cooking were sternly rebuked. "I eat only twice a day; that's as often as you will eat," he told one hungry visitor. "Eating only irritates the stomach and eating twice a day irritates it less than three times a day."[40] "I notice that my good cooking and eating friends are all dead or dieing," he told Flora. "As an example of how I live, I roasted a shoulder of venison a week ago and have made some tea and had a raw onion or some slaw and a biscuit with it twice a day."[41] He ate most of his vegetables raw. Trevor Davis, a friend from Juneau, remembered anchoring up in Mole Harbor once during a hunting trip:

Hasselborg came out to the boat in the afternoon and brought several bunches of turnips, carrots and some other vegetables. He gave them to us and we talked for a while. We gave him some food in return, you know, and he left. The next day he came back and he said, 'Well, how did you like the turnips?' and I said, 'Oh, those were fine turnips, we did them just right.' And Hasselborg said, 'Did you *cook* those turnips?!' He was kind of peeved. He wouldn't think of cooking turnips or carrots.[42]

Visitors who stayed on their boats often invited him out to eat with them, but he almost always declined. Even when they hired him as a guide, he preferred to sleep on shore. "I wanted to go ashore with my dirty rags and sleep under a tree at night," he told Flora after a couple from California insisted that he sleep in a spare stateroom on their seventy-foot yacht. "The first morning, Mrs. [Stewart Edward] White asked me how the bed was. I said it was just as good as sleeping under a tree. She said that is a great compliment."[43]

By the end of July, when Hasselborg was often busiest with visitors and his garden, the salmon were beginning to spawn in Mole River. Bald eagles on the lookout for a meal perched in the spruce and hemlock along the stream, and his bears were all around, sometimes as many as four or five visible at once from the cabin window. Solitary animals most of the year, they now competed for the best fishing spots. Differences of opinion rarely came to fights, though there were many fast exits and entrances, complicated maneuverings for position, and growling and huffing as the social order was sorted out. Eager for their first solid meal in many months, they fished with methodical intensity, stalking slowly through the shallows, then galloping off in a storm of water in hot pursuit of a fish. In a few hours, an adult could catch and eat a dozen salmon. They kept at it most of the day; even in the dusky light near midnight, Hasselborg could hear them splashing and see their phantom shapes moving along the river.

View of Mt. Distik from Hasselborg Lake, 1986. *Photograph by J. Howe*

By September, the grass beside the river was beaten down and littered with salmon bones, and the stench of dead fish hung in the air. The bears had begun to move back up into the mountains as bright flocks of shorebirds swept through Mole Harbor, headed south after nesting on the tundra. Hundreds of robins flew in to feast on maggots in the rotten salmon Hasselborg forked up onto his garden. One year he reported that three hundred robins had enjoyed his maggots so much they had decided to spend the fall at Mole Harbor; they were singing all at once, he said, and the ground was covered with feathers where they had been fighting.[44] Another year, he guessed he had put up about three thousand salmon and joked about how that meant he would have thirty million maggots to feed about a thousand robins. "I put the fish up for my robins as much as for the garden," he told Flora.[45]

As fall came in, darkness crept close around the days and it rained, sometimes for days without stopping. Having lived in southeast Alaska for so many years, in his journals Hasselborg distinguished between three kinds of wet weather: "raynaldai," "drizlaldai," and "sprinks."[46] He canned vegetables and dug up his beets, carrots, onions, turnips, and potatoes, storing them in a root cellar behind the cabin. He preserved strawberries and raspberries from his garden and wild currants and blueberries from the forest.[47] He patched the cabin roof. Day after day, laying in wood for the winter, he wrote "chopn" in his journal.[48]

Usually by October the first dusting of snow had appeared high on Mt. Distik. He went hunting as soon as the snow had chased the deer down below the tree line, and it was cold enough that meat wouldn't spoil too quickly. He always looked forward to getting away from his chores for a while, walking the woods in the gathering stillness of late fall. It was the only hunting he did now, and he had it down to an exact science. One year, he said he used eight bullets to kill eight bucks with a .25 caliber rifle.[49] In his journals, he recorded a successful hunt as "sumeet" (some meat) followed by "butcherin" and "kanning."[50]

The coldest winters arrived early, by November—relentless, thick snowfalls alternating with piercing cold, sparkling clear days when the sky burned deep blue behind snow-capped mountains towering all around. The north wind roared down Seymour Canal, whipping storms of spray whirling hundreds of feet in the air, blowing snow off the top of Mt. Distik; the temperature dropped below freezing for weeks at a time, Mole River froze solid, and snow drifted to the cabin eaves. Many winters were milder, however. Some years, it stayed so warm he would

One of Allen Hasselborg's lean-to's in mountains of Admiralty Island.
Courtesy of P. Sheppard

come across a bear who thought it was still fall, nosing around his woodshed late in December. The temperature could stay above freezing most of the time, and his flowers would bloom and his cabbages keep growing almost until spring.

During the winter, even more than the other seasons, he was wrapped up alone in the moist stillness of Admiralty Island. Shut in by darkness for as much as eighteen hours a day, for months at a time he saw no one and might hear only one or two boats go by in the distance. In a letter to his family late one fall, he said he was about to "hibernate," enclosing the word in quotes perhaps so they wouldn't think he was beginning to act too much like a bear, perhaps so as not to suggest idleness.[51] He wasn't like some old-timers he knew who spent most of the winter in bed, he said; he trapped during the winter, and that kept him busy enough.

He usually ran about thirty traps, some up at the lakes for beaver, others in the forest for mink, marten, and weasel. Some years, he had lines up to the Gambier Bay divide, along the east flank of Mt. Distik, and near the headwaters of Mole River. He tried to check his traps regularly, so he was usually out all day every day, tramping on snowshoes for hours through the woods. At the lakes and near the top of Mole River, he had crude shelters—poles leaned against fallen trees, roofed with moss and slabs of wood—where he could camp if he got caught out late or the weather turned bad. In his journals, "skinz" summed up a day spent skinning his catch, scraping the pelts and stretching them out on boards to dry.[52]

Other than trapping and his daily chores, he didn't have much to do during the winter. That left a lot of time for reading—not that reading was a casual pastime. He read with the same precise determination he applied to shooting a deer or planting his garden, convinced, like his father, that he could learn anything on his own, given enough time and self-discipline. He firmly believed that compulsory education was second only to the "pretense" of religion as the main cause of the world's problems.[53] "I don't suppose you know how prejudiced I am about education," he wrote Flora at one point. "It is about 55 years ago that I kicked the shins of Minerva O'Brien and I feel the same way about education yet. W. Woodrow Wilson went to school until he was 34, and we are still paying for it—$40,000,000,000. . . . I don't mind anyone *learning* all they can, but this compulsory teaching of nitwits and lazy ones is making a fool of the country."[54]

His library was stocked with dozens of books about hunting, exploration, history, botany, and geology, a complete set of Shakespeare's plays, a *Webster's Dictionary*, and a thirty-volume *Encyclopedia Britannica*. At one time or another, his family and friends gave him subscriptions to *Scientific American, The Literary Digest, Alaska Sportsman, National Geographic*, and several other magazines and scientific journals. It mattered to him that what he read was absolutely factual, which meant books on scientific subjects, true stories about hunting and exploration (preferably in Alaska) and the encyclopedia.[55] With the distinct exception of Shakespeare's plays, everything else was "fiction," and he had little use for it. Flora occasionally gave him novels about Alaska, and they never failed to disappoint him. "The trouble with all the fictionists is they don't know anything about what they are writing about," he told her at one point.[56] He particularly disliked the work of James Oliver Curwood, whom he accused of "getting up" several "faked" novels about Alaska. Alaskans were so offended by them, he said, that if Curwood ever dared show his face in Juneau, he would be "mobbed and thrown off the dock."[57] He called another novel Flora sent him "a horrible scandalous yarn," complaining that he might have to use all the buttons in his sewing box to keep the characters straight.[58]

Even worse than novelists, though, were the "fictionists"[59]—writers who pretended to know something about Alaska wildlife. They came up from the states, traveled around a bit, then published books and articles full of errors. William W. Wright, for example, the author of a popular book about bears, made himself out to be an expert, though Hasselborg knew for a fact that he had encountered only about a dozen bears in the wild. Even *Travels in Alaska*, a book by the famous naturalist John Muir, had "a great many little natural history mistakes," he said.[60] No book could be completely trusted, not even the encyclopedia. His eleven-volume set looked pretty ragged, several visitors noticed, as he had spent many long winter evenings hunting for mistakes and contradictions and correcting them with sharp jabs of his pencil. When a friend offered him a new one, he firmly refused, explaining that it had taken him twenty years to correct the one he had.[61]

"We had a pretty stiff old fashioned winter but the grass is beginning to come and the robins and other South birds are arriving," he wrote Flora early one spring. "I am looking over my seeds ect. which have arrived. Am planting the acre of old ground to clover. If I put it in strawberries would have to start a 'cannery,' as some of the homesteaders are doing …. but I depend on spuds."[62] When spring arrived, his first order of business was a trip to town.

"Hasselborg had it figured out," a friend remembered. "Time was nothing to him. "He'd line up and study the weather and then start out."[63] Usually he waited for a high tide so he could float out through the channel he kept dredged in the river. After rounding Point Hugh, he was exposed to miles of open water in Stephens Passage, so he ran close along the eastern shore of Admiralty Island, past sheer cliffs and promontories and steep, rocky beaches. The *Bulldogg* could buck fairly heavy seas, but if

Point Hugh, Admiralty Island, looking across entrance to Seymour Canal, 1984. *Photograph by J. Howe*

he took a skiff and it got rough, he'd have to head for shore and camp until the water settled down. Once in early March, he was hit by high winds and temperatures down to four degrees, and it took him two weeks to get to town. Often he camped behind the beach south of Station Point, or in Doty Cove, before running the rest of the way in.

People in Juneau remember that Hasselborg usually smelled pretty smoky by the time he got to town. If it was March or April and no one had seen him for a while, his arrival was a sure sign of spring; if it was late fall, they were reminded that winter was coming. "First thing he'd do when he hit town is go to the barbershop," a friend recalled. "He was a man who'd get his business done and get going."[64] After selling his furs, picking up his mail at the post office, and exchanging books at the library, he went shopping for staples like flour, tea, sugar, salt, and rice. Occasionally he splurged on fresh fruit, butter, or eggs. He also bought ammunition, gas and oil for his boats, perhaps a tool he needed or seeds for his garden, paying with crumpled bills he pulled from several different pockets. He often said there wasn't much in town he wanted or needed to buy. Once he was spotted leaving for several months with only a small box under his arm. Another year, he left for the winter after spending a total of eight dollars on food, ammunition, and a new pair of socks. He never ate in restaurants and always slept on his boat, never in a hotel. One friend remembered going down to the harbor to visit him late one fall and finding him asleep in his skiff under a tarp covered with four inches of snow.

In between errands, he returned to his boat and tried to answer all his mail. He might have as many as a dozen letters to write. The longest were no more than two pages. He frequently reminded his correspondents that writing was hard work. "Well I cant write with a pen as I only write once in two or three months and do too much chopping ect. between times," he warned his family one year.[65] Many Alaskans, except bureaucrats, of course, had the same problem, he said. "There are actually thousands of men who drift up this coast every year. Some of them go all the way to Siberia or the Arctic and Hudson Bay, and they get all out of the habit of writing. Some of them may be doctors, ect., but you wouldent think they had ever been to school."[66]

He often got requests for specimens from naturalists in the states, and when he felt like it, he obliged them. When Dixon asked for a plaster cast of the biggest bear paw print he could find, he sent down a twelve-inch print he found in his garden.

For Dixon and the other naturalists from the Alexander Expeditions, his letters must have come like quick blasts of fresh air. "Just got in from a hard old winter at the ranch," he wrote Swarth one spring.

> The rabbits all died in the interior last year and the lynx and owls all came to the coast the last two years. They have almost cleaned up the grouse and ptarmigans, and the lynx are doing well on mallards. Last fall I shot three bubos [great horned owls] around the house and a visitor shot one that had just killed a mink. Louis Magg who is a very reliable man was trapping around Teg Point last fall and winter. He said he killed more than twenty owls with clubs or by throwing his trapping hatchet at them. He saw a great many more, some sitting around hooting in daylight. One that he killed was eating a loon not dead yet on the beach, one was eating a gull alive. One was eating a squirrel. One was eating another owl which was not dead yet. One was eating a mink, and mink were very scarce, supposed to have been killed off by owls. He found an eagle eating one owl, and I saw at a deer carcass where an eagle, I supposed, had killed and eaten a white owl.[67]

Within his own family, Flora and Ebba were his best correspondents. He sent them jelly preserves, pressed flowers, and roots and seeds of plants with detailed growing instructions. Once he sent Ebba a pair of Admiralty Island toads to donate to the Bureau of Fisheries Aquarium in Washington, D.C.[68]

In a typical letter to his sisters, his news rushed out in fits and starts with requests for the latest on the Hasselborg family. He enjoyed teasing Flora about Florida: it was too hot, there were too many diseases, and judging by the pictures she sent him, her vegetables were worse than any grown on the poorest soil in Alaska.

He liked to remind her that their brother Ira had been disabled by hookworm, a tropical parasite, soon after the family moved to Florida and that Flora herself had several bouts with malaria. "I don't think much of your sunny south," he told her, "There will be a lot of queer things left after you have got ridd of malaria and hookworms."[69] The Pacific Northwest was the only country, he said. "I couldent live in a country that had no mountains or scenery or climate. Florida never had a climate and you don't know it."[70]

To his sisters' children, he was a fond, if absent-minded uncle. "Got your letter some time ago," he wrote Flora one year. "Was surprised to hear your boys were so old and that one of them was a girl."[71] He sent them furs, flower seeds, and tips on how to attract wild animals and catch frogs. When they were older, he counseled them about their schooling and finding work. Flora named a son after him, and he took special pleasure in sending advice to "Namesake," particularly when little Allen joined the Boy Scouts and developed an interest in guns and hunting. While his nephew Raymond was in college studying entomology, Uncle Allen mailed him some strange-looking insects with a request for a full report.

> I am sending a bottle of bugs from three heads
> of lettuce. . . . Brown color, fat body, 6 legs, no
> head, a double snout and two horns. I want to know
> about them. Have had lots of good lettuce for 6
> weeks. Put my specks on a few days ago and found
> the lettuce was full of these mites. They had been

biting my mouth. Must have eaten several hundred of them. . . . What will they do to me? They are pretty tough. I laid some on a board and had to hit them several times with a club to kill them.[72]

By the next spring, Raymond hadn't yet answered his request. "You have never told me anything about those wonderfull mites I sent you. If you had used a magnifier you would have seen they were something extra. I wanted to know the genus and species and what they are doing to my insides. Dont want to know how to kill them. I would get you a lot more next summer but doubt if I will ever see one again. They all dissapeared after I got that lot."[73]

When Raymond finally responded, Hasselborg was amused to learn that no one knew much about them. He was still wondering what they might do to him and guessed they had already chewed from his stomach to the top of his head. He was annoyed that Raymond's professor hadn't appreciated them: "I am still feeling bad about those wonderful mites that you gave to some bum expert or 'Doctor' or whichever. They were the only ones of their kind, and it was a great loss to science when that bum Dr. threw them in the slop bucket."[74]

Catching up on correspondence was among the least of Hasselborg's concerns when he was in town, however. "You cant imagine what a fuss I am in when I do come to town and forget half the things I came for even," he wrote Flora one spring.[75] Once he went in just to buy seeds for his garden and was halfway home before he realized he'd forgotten them. "I have fits all the time and think I am lucky to get grub and gas and get out," he fumed after another hectic trip.[76] "I don't see anybody when I am out home for months and get all mixed up when I come to the city.

There is 117 busy autos in this little town and the streets are only 20 ft. wide, so you can imagine how nervous they make an old rancher."[77] Even worse than autos were the "fool aquaplanes."[78] He was disappointed one year when one of Flora's sons developed an interest in aviation. "Gas boats are bad enough, autos are an invention of the devil, and airplanes are worse," he warned her.[79]

Though all the people and cars in the streets never failed to rattle him, most of his fits occurred in the offices of the Biological Survey and the Territorial Game Department. He paid two dollars for a trapping license every year and tried to obey the regulations, so it infuriated him when he couldn't sell the pelt of an animal caught accidentally in a trap he'd set for a legal species. Or he would come in and discover a regulation had been changed during the winter, and he had either trapped out of season or missed an open season that had profited other trappers. He was always sure the bureaucrats and local furriers were in cahoots to defraud him with low prices and by sending "fur pirates"[80] out to trap illegally.

In the early 1920s, after discovering evidence of poachers up at the Admiralty Island lakes, Hasselborg hurried into town to protest. Probably as a peace offering, someone in the Game Department appointed him fur warden at Mole Harbor. Deputy Hasselborg soon found fresh sign of the poachers and called up a posse. "I was right to the front with blood in my eye and toting an old Colt," he wrote a friend a few weeks later.[81] They had arrested seven of the poachers, all of them Indians, but three others had escaped. Hasselborg was furious when local missionaries got the culprits out of jail. He was sure they returned to Admiralty in time to finish off all the mink before the season opened.[82]

During the period between 1929 and 1949, Hasselborg averaged about three trips into Juneau every year. Usually he stayed no more than two or three days; occasionally his disputes with the government kept him longer. A storm might also postpone his departure, though then he often went down to the end of Gastineau Channel to camp until the weather lifted. One spring, he spent ten days waiting for the *Bulldogg's* engine to get rebored and four more days breaking it in with elbow grease. Sometimes he came in to meet hunters or photographers who had hired him as a guide and was delayed if they didn't arrive on time.

In his journals, the dates when he is in town are noticeably blank. You can almost hear his sigh of relief the day he gets home: "JunotoMole . . . homagain."[83]

9

BEAR MAN

WITH ONLY A FEW hours remaining before the steamer left for Seattle, Harold Coolidge began a long letter to his father. "August 4, 1925, . . . Hotel Zynda, . . . Juneau, Alaska. . . ." After a month on Admiralty Island with Hasselborg, the young Harvard student was having a hard time concentrating. "I can't keep my mind focused tonight, it's so funny to be back."

> Harsilborg [*sic*] is a real "old timer." He has a wonderful black beard, is a man of medium height, and as strong as an ox. . . . It is a very exceptional thing to spend a month with a man so intelligent in all lines. He has got the science of bear hunting learned perfectly, and got us so we could smell bear often before we saw them. He knows his birds, animals, plants, fish and rocks. He is a gardener, and a wonderful boatman, not to mention packer and guide. He has never ridden in an automobile, and never will. He has only used a telephone once, and then he broke it. He hates town because walking on hard streets hurts his feet. The

ground on Admiralty Island is all soft and all up
and down. We were really out of touch entirely for
a month except for one fisherman we checked our
date from. When we went into the interior of
the island no one knew our whereabouts. H.
[Hasselborg] is the only person who could find his
way, as it is all unexplored.[1]

A concise portrait of Hasselborg at age forty-eight, it was also
a typical reaction from people he took into the Admiralty wilderness in the years between 1925 and 1935, when he most active as
a guide. They all were intrigued by the crusty woodsman who
knew so much about Admiralty Island and its bears—the independent, hard-working homesteader; the solitary, reserved
bachelor with a sharp wit who ruled Mole Harbor like a king.

Most of Hasselborg's hunting parties were from the states:
wealthy businessmen, college students on summer vacation,
scientists collecting specimens, sportsmen after trophies. Some
were skilled marksmen and competent outdoorsmen; others were
poor shots and clumsy in the woods, happy just to return home
with a bearskin rug to impress their friends. A few were like Harold
Coolidge: young men yearning for adventure.

Perhaps because he was a cousin of President Calvin Coolidge,
Harold Coolidge had been able to secure an assignment from the
U.S. Biological Survey to collect bear specimens on Admiralty
Island that summer of 1925. He and a Harvard classmate, Charles
Day, had arrived early in July, before many bears were down on
the salmon streams. "After a day at Hasselborg's shack, we packed
up a tent, blankets, tea, salt and flour to go up to Hasselborg Lake
in the interior," Coolidge told his father. "Charles' and my pack
weighed about 40 pounds and Hasselborg's about 70. It was darned
hard work climbing through thick devil's club over a pass 1,000

Charles Day, Admiralty Island, 1925. *Courtesy of H. Coolidge*

feet high and rather steep. Going was so hard it took five hours to go three miles."

At Lake Alexander, they launched a canoe Hasselborg kept stashed there and paddled nine miles, with one portage, to the far end of Hasselborg Lake.[2] "We figured on shooting a deer the first day, but Charlie missed the only shot we had at a buck," Coolidge wrote. He hunted alone on the way back to camp and got lost. "Once lost in these woods in the rain, Hasselborg says you are as good as dead, but I had given Charles my compass and he managed to strike the lake just at dark and was dead exhausted, torn by devil's club, and a wiser man when we got him in." By then they were all weak from living for several days on hot cakes and tea; Day was so exhausted he could barely move. Hasselborg said he would rather starve than shoot a doe that might have a fawn, so he and Coolidge climbed three thousand feet up above timberline to look for bucks. Coolidge shot a yearling, but the meat lasted only a few days. All the while it had been raining steadily and clouds had obscured their view of the mountains, so when they ran out of flour they packed up and returned to Mole Harbor.

After a day or two of rest and eating their fill of Hasselborg's vegetables and strawberries, they bushwhacked two days up into the mountains behind Mt. Distik. At two thousand feet, they made camp on a grassy saddle between two taller ridges. "Our situation was a splendid one," Coolidge wrote. "Hasselborg had been there once, but no one else ever that he had heard of. . . . We made wooden spoons and lived a week on venison roasted on a stick, with tea and mush thrown in."

Looking for bear one day, they spotted a handsome one with a yellow back and black legs on a mountain to the south. They climbed over to it the next morning. Coolidge and Day fired at the same time from about two hundred yards away, dropping it in its

"Yellow bear" collected for U.S. Biological Survey by Harold Coolidge and
Charles Day, Admiralty Island, 1925. *Courtesy of H. Coolidge*

tracks. "It was not a large bear, but we got a real thrill out of
him," Coolidge said. They photographed it, skinned it, and took
its skull. That night they cut big, juicy steaks off the carcass.
"Being very hungry, we agreed not to bite into our individual
steaks until a given signal, and when we did so, we spat the meat
out and made terrible faces as it tasted like putrid fish. By bad
luck, that particular yellow bear had fed on salmon before going
after blueberries at a higher altitude. I assure you, there is
nothing more horrible than biting into a juicy steak that tastes
like decayed salmon."[3]

Shortly thereafter, Hasselborg decided that most of the bears
had moved lower, so they went back to Mole Harbor, traveling

the ten-mile distance in less than a day. On the way down, they came across many bear tracks and piles of fresh dung. "H. was constantly scared going through the brush," Coolidge said. "If you come on a brown bear suddenly, he will go for you, especially if wounded. H. had an arm half chewed off by one. This constant alertness with gun cocked, and a heavy pack, was tiresome."[4]

By then the salmon were beginning to arrive, so they went out in the *Bulldogg* to hunt the creeks along Seymour Canal. It was the most dangerous sort of hunting, Coolidge said, wading through water up to their knees, stumbling on slippery rocks, with big salmon constantly bumping against their legs. Most of the time, the wind carried their scent upstream, spooking the bears, though one calm evening they saw twenty-seven in two hours, more than Hasselborg had ever seen in one day. "We didn't fire a shot as they were none of them the very big bear we wanted for our last ones," Coolidge wrote.

Finally, on their fourth day out, they ran into a big bear wading downstream toward them. Coolidge broke its back with his first shot, but it took four more to "flatten him out." They skinned it the next day, an unpleasant task due to the flies and the rain, which threatened to damage the pelt.

> The next night we were hunting up a creek sneaking along on our stomachs in the brush . . . having already run 7 bear, when we spotted a large yellow colored bear. We were making a sneak to get a shot at him when we almost ran into a good sized brown in the middle of the creek. The old boy was not as big as the yellow, and yet we couldn't get by him, and didn't want to shoot him. We were in a most awkward situation, mixed up in alders, and if he charged, we all knew there'd be

a hot time of it for we'd get all tangled up in the bushes and guns. There was no time for hesitation, he had our wind before we came onto him. He was fighting mad, and on seeing us, did charge. H. had often warned us of how little time it takes these fellows to cover ground. He never got beyond his first jump, although he dropped only a few feet in front of us. Charlie and I fired simultaneously, and both hit him. The big magnum bullet found a vital spot and had such shocking power that with Charlie's it stopped him. H. has put 8 shots into one bear, and had him reach him in a charge before he dropped him with a ninth, and in that case all that was left of the bear was a bag of bones.

We cut off his head and I took the scientific measurements. It was getting dark fast and we had to get out of this creek that had too many bears before we ran on some more. We got back to our skiff to find such a stiff squall blowing that she could hardly live in it, with H. alone in the skiff. Chas. and I walked along the shore and watched H. fight the wind, standing in the skiff with a pole. He had one mile of flats with shallow white caps to negotiate, and he made it beautifully.[5]

His hunt with Hasselborg would prove to be a turning point in Coolidge's life. That fall at Harvard, he changed his major to zoology and went on to a long and distinguished career as a zoologist and wildlife conservationist. He would correspond faithfully with Hasselborg for the next thirty years, often reminiscing about Admiralty Island and its bears, obviously very fond of the "real old timer" who had taken him to them.

Harold Coolidge (left) and Allen Hasselborg, Admiralty Island, 1925.
Photograph by C. Day. Courtesy of H. Coolidge

Hasselborg had a fine time on that hunt, too. Coolidge and Day had been a little green in the woods but eager to learn. He had shown them some of his favorite country and helped them collect three respectable specimens. They had also named two mountains behind Mole Harbor: Botany Peak, where they had camped for a week, and Yellow Bear Mountain, where Coolidge and Day shot their first bear.[6] It had been like the old days when he guided Annie Alexander.

Many of the parties Hasselborg guided in the late twenties and early thirties weren't after trophies or museum specimens. They were photographers—conservationists from below who were working on films and magazine stories, tourists after snapshots for the folks back home, professionals from Juneau. The Juneau people came down to Mole Harbor on their own and pretty much knew what they were doing, while most of the others needed transportation and a lot of help staying out of trouble with the bears. Usually he took them up Mole River, south to Gambier Bay, or north to the salmon streams along Seymour Canal. At the mouths of most of the creeks they could set up their camera tripods behind tall grass and see a good distance in every direction. Often they had to sit patiently for hours, watching and waiting, before a bear showed up. Hasselborg passed the time either stretched out asleep with his hat over his eyes or sitting quietly observing wildlife with what one photographer described as "keen, scientific alertness. . . . Nothing escaped his eyes as he studied and enjoyed the wilderness. His eyes seemed to brighten as he studied the life around him."[7]

Camera hunting bears was often more difficult and risky than hunting bears with a rifle. "You had to get close to get good shots," recalled one photographer. "No doubt about it, Hasselborg got me close! I was terrified, but I tried not to show it."[8] Out near the mouths of the streams, they might spend hours filming and photographing bears fishing. Each bear had a different technique. Some stood in the shallows, peering intently into the water, waiting for a salmon to swim within reach. Others raced up and down, furiously chasing every fish in sight. The more relaxed ones lolled about in deep pools, dunking their heads under to look for a meal. They all seemed to have such distinctive personalities and seemed so human, especially when they stood up on their hind legs to spot fish or sniff the breeze, it was easy to give them names. Out near the beach, most were adult males, though occasionally a female with cubs ventured out of the woods. Usually the cubs either sat on the bank like kids in school,

Brown bear, Admiralty Island, 1931. From the film, *The Great Bear of Alaska* by William Finley and Arthur Pack (American Nature Association). *Courtesy of Oregon Historical Society*

watching the adults fish, or scampered about chasing gulls and ravens and anything else that moved. Most of the time, the bears ignored the photographers, or pretended to: catching salmon was far more important to them than a few humans who didn't seem threatening. Still, they didn't like being startled or crowded. If one came too close, Hasselborg would stand up and tell everyone to stand up, too, so the bear could see them and decide what to do next. Often a bear that approached them was either curious or confused—unable to form an opinion until it got a good look at them or caught their scent.

Late one morning in August 1929, Hasselborg and John Holzworth, a lawyer from New York, sat hidden behind tall grass at the mouth of Swan Creek.

They waited two hours before a bear came rushing into view in hot pursuit of a salmon. It pounced, picked the fish up in its jaws, and stalked off into the forest. The wind changed direction, and they were just beginning to think the bear had smelled them, when suddenly it reappeared. Holzworth grabbed a camera and crept closer. Hasselborg followed, rifle in one hand, Holzworth's other camera in the other.[9] The bear started back down the creek toward them, stopping now and then to peer into the water. When only about fifteen yards away, it climbed up on a log to reconnoiter.

"The pose was a majestic and beautiful one, with the vari-colored green alders and willows behind him, and the swiftly running water at his feet," Holzworth wrote later.

> It was thrilling to watch him through the finder and to hear the soft purr of the little motors. I knew that his every action and movement was being taken perfectly, for the light was fine and the natural color film was recording all the natural beauty of the background. A full quarter of a minute he stood poised, with his head and neck stretched up and towards us. Then, having reasoned the matter out, he turned around on the log, and made a few quick bounds into the depths of the spruce timber.[10]

Camera hunting upstream was much more nerve-wracking than photographing bears near the beach. The forest closed in like a jungle, the water rushed loudly, and often you couldn't see more than a few yards in any direction. Hasselborg led the way,

137

Allen Hasselborg guiding Arthur Pack on camera hunt for bears, Admiralty Island, 1931. *Courtesy of Oregon Historical Society*

usually carrying a pack full of camera equipment. "Our guide seemed to know every hidden and projecting rock beneath the surface of the tumbling water, and stepped easily from one foot-hold to another, while we stumbled behind him," remembered Arthur Pack, a conservationist from Washington, D.C.[11] "He carefully plucked off every frond of fern or branch of devil's club or alder that might brush against us, to kill our scent, and always had us step upon bare rocks or in the water, and, after crossing fallen logs without touching them with our hands, to splash them with water to wash off any possible scent."[12]

When the water got too deep or a downed tree blocked their way, they detoured into the forest. Holzworth recalled forcing his way through devil's club so thick he couldn't see more than three feet in any direction, when suddenly, very close by, a peculiar, blood-curdling moan began.

> It continued with increasing volume, a passionate and frenzied warning. It seemed to come from all sides; evidently the bear was working himself up to a heated fury, but I could not tell where he might emerge. Slowly and simultaneously both of us backed from the narrow cul-de-sac in which we were thus trapped. The first minute the moan sounded precisely like the wail which a teller of a ghost story in a dark room uses to terrify his listeners. But after a minute other tones joined; the note became deeper and deeper, until it sounded like the basso profundo of the Anvil Chorus in *Toreador*. For fully five minutes this unseen quartette of bears filled the forest with the growls of their outraged indignation. With rifle poised for instant action, the Old Man waited; he had two extra cartridges between the fingers of his left hand that could have been inserted into the rifle a second after firing the shots already in place.
>
> But our slow retreat must have had the desired effect. Gradually the moans ceased and fifteen minutes after they had first commenced, we turned the corner of the creek and went on.[13]

Often the bears seemed to be playing tricks. One would suddenly appear upstream, vanish into the forest, then reappear downstream moments later, acting thoroughly nonchalant. Their games could suddenly turn deadly serious, however, especially if the main player was a sow with cubs. Holzworth almost learned that lesson the hard way one afternoon when he and Hasselborg came upon a sow and her cub on a gravel bar contentedly eating a salmon. Holzworth got some good shots from about seventy-five yards away before the sow began wading upstream with the cub loping along the bar beside her. They didn't seem to notice when Holzworth began following them. Soon they disappeared behind a bend in the river, and by the time Holzworth came around it they were nowhere in sight. Noticing a wet spot on the bar where they had climbed into the forest, he waded out into deeper water and started upstream again. Just then, he happened to turn to look for his guide and was startled to see Hasselborg stopped about forty yards back, waving frantically at him.[14]

"From my position in the rear, I could see something he couldn't," Hasselborg said later. "Besides, I thought I knew what that old lady was up to."[15] He had seen her hustle her cub up a tree and return to the stream to set an ambush. "The bear was no more than fifteen yards from him, on her haunches behind a blowdown stump," Hasselborg said. "Her teeth were showing, and she was licking her tongue and working her jaws. The photographer didn't see her, and it's a good thing he didn't, because the instant their eyes met I think she would have ripped him to pieces. . . ."[16]

Males were usually more easygoing than females with cubs. The same day the sow tried to ambush Holzworth, a big boar suddenly materialized on the trail in front of them, shot a casual glance their way, then strolled on ahead to a small hemlock, stood on its hind legs, and reached up to rip off a long strip of bark. Then it dropped down and gave them a long, hard look before swaggering off into the forest. "He'd left his brand high enough so I could barely reach it with the extended muzzle of my rifle," Hasselborg said. "The big fellow didn't want to fight; he just wanted to warn us what we'd be up against if *we* started one."[17]

The Admiralty bears had been hunted for years and knew humans could be dangerous, though many still didn't keep their distance. They liked to throw their weight around, let you know who was boss. Hasselborg did what he could to stay out of their way, and gave them every opportunity to identify him. If they insisted on raising the stakes, however, it was a serious mistake to back down, as they were often just bluffing. Arthur Pack described Hasselborg facing down an ill-tempered female who challenged them as they were walking up a stream:

> She stood on her hind legs in the water, only ten yards away, growling and weaving from side to side. Hers was no comical face. Her long grizzly nose wrinkled up in a snarl. Her eyes were hard and full of hatred. She watched the man with the gun [Hasselborg], who stared back at her steadily and intently. Suddenly, for the third time on our trip, the courage and confidence of our experienced guide won out. The grizzly dropped to all fours, but her head was not down for a charge. She edged slowly out of the water at the opposite bank, growling and pausing from time to time, as if about to turn and attack. Then, rumbling, she stalked off into the bushes.[18]

Bears liked to have the last word, Hasselborg told Pack. Maintaining their dignity was important to them, he often said. Some weren't open to negotiation, though, and had to be firmly discouraged from charging. One afternoon on a tide flat in Seymour Canal, Pack and a companion witnessed Hasselborg's favorite technique. They had spotted a bear in the distance and were walking toward it, when suddenly it launched an offensive. "Fifty yards, forty yards—thirty; straight toward the camera-laden trio came the grizzly, snarling as he rushed," Pack wrote later.

> Hasselborg . . . brought his gun to his shoulder for action. He barked a sharp command. 'Stop that, boy! Stop it! Stop it quick!' If his words had been bullets, they could not have been more effective. Slithering and sliding on the beach, the huge animal brought up short, shaking his head in surprise.... Across ninety feet of mud and mussels in the gathering dusk, the three humans and one thousand pounds of disconcerted grizzly stared at each other.
>
> Suddenly, the spurt of courage that had inspired his charge deserted the bear. He turned tail and ran a few yards, then stopped to gaze sulkily back at the trio, as if debating his course. Then he slowly walked toward the shore, punctuating his retreat with glowering looks at his conquerors. At a safe distance, he paused to scratch himself nonchalantly—as if to show he wasn't afraid, then continued his lumbering gait to the edge of the beach. There he sat down, dog-like, to watch.[19]

Several other photographers saw Hasselborg stop bears that way. Without waving his arms or moving suddenly, he would hold his ground and quietly but firmly tell them to go back. Trevor Davis remembered being out with Hasselborg once and coming upon a female.

Brown Bear, Admiralty Island, 1930s. *Photograph by A. Hasselborg. Courtesy of Alaska Historical Library*

Hasselborg had a double-barrel elephant gun and he had it pointed at the bear and he was talking to her. He says, 'You go back! You go back now! Go back!' She was sitting down on her haunches, and she was pawing the ground and snapping her teeth and my hair started going up because the bear was only about thirty or forty feet away. Pretty soon, sure enough, she turned around and walked off.[20]

Bears were surprised and puzzled by the sound of the human voice and would hold everything, including a full charge, while they sorted things out. Almost anything could divert them.

Frank and Eleanor Hibben, a couple from New Mexico, recalled walking back to Hasselborg's skiff after a day of filming when a dark shape suddenly loomed up ahead of them on the beach. Hasselborg, in the lead as usual, stopped and flung out an arm so quickly the two tired photographers piled into him. Now the bear was coming straight toward them in a fast, deliberate walk, ears laid back, head low and swinging from side to side. As Hibben raised his rifle to his shoulder, he realized that Hasselborg wasn't even trying to talk to the bear; it was too late for verbal negotiation. Hasselborg snatched off his canvas hat and flung it at the bear, hitting it in the face. The bear reared back, startled, then eased over and began sniffing at a wad of chewing gum stuck to the top of the hat. Its curiosity aroused, it reached out cautiously with one paw and flipped the hat over. Reacting to a sudden, strong whiff of human scent, it ripped at the hat with its claws, then pounced on a torn piece and bounced up and down on it with both front paws until the scrap disappeared into the mud. That annoyed Hasselborg, so he picked up a rock about the size of a grapefruit and threw it at the bear with a yell that sounded to Hibben like "you slobbering slob!" The rock bounced once and struck the huge animal full on the nose. The bear shied away, then reared back, distracted by the rock. Hasselborg motioned the Hibbens toward the edge of the water. The bear was still staring at the rock as the photographers waded cautiously past and walked quickly to the skiff. "I told you they were all foolish bears," Hasselborg scoffed as they headed back to Mole Harbor.[21]

Every so often even a good scolding or diversionary tactic didn't work. Then, Hasselborg was always ready with his rifle. Amos Burg, a photographer from Juneau, remembered a sow with three cubs that ignored Hasselborg's verbal warning and charged full speed toward them. Hasselborg had to fire several shots into the gravel in front of her before she turned aside, only about a hundred feet from them. "I didn't want to shoot her," he told Burg. "I was thinking of those three cubs."[22]

During his years as a hunter for Alexander and Merriam, Hasselborg had been charged about a dozen times, so he was confident that he could read a bear's signals and protect himself and his parties if need be. Bears were often unpredictable, as different one from another as people, he said. And they were curious, like ravens; they liked to watch people.[23] If you didn't threaten or embarrass them, they usually behaved, though sometimes curiosity, confusion, or a bad temper got the best of them, and then you had be firm with them.[24] "It doesn't do any good to try to bluff a bear, because he savvies too much," he told Holzworth. "If a bear starts for you, be firm with him and tell him to go back; above anything else, don't start running unless you are sure of a tree."[25] During the ten years he was busiest guiding photographers, he fired warning shots only a few times. He didn't like raising his voice with bears; raising his gun to his shoulder only meant that diplomacy had failed. When Holzworth described him shouting and pointing his rifle at a bear, Hasselborg angrily corrected him: "This bear came to within 12 feet. [I] never had a rifle to my shoulder [on that trip] and never hollered at a bear always spoke quietly."[26]

By the time he wrote those words, it was 1939 and he had quit guiding altogether. What had been a way to make some money and get out into the country to see bears had become annoying, frustrating work he could easily do without. Much of the blame for his disappointment he would lay squarely on John Holzworth, the New York lawyer who lured him into a national political battle over Admiralty Island and its bears.

10

WISE IN HIS

JUDGMENT

ALTHOUGH HASSELBORG had properly applied for his Mole Harbor homestead and had been proving up on it for several years, the government was reluctant to give him title to the land. "Am maybe getting a patent to my homestead and have had the whole Alaska bureaucrat government on the run and sweating blood," he wrote Flora in 1923.[1] Some Forest Service rangers had tried to evict him from Mole Harbor, and he had fired at their boat as soon as it came within range of his .405. When the rangers asked the U.S. Marshall in Juneau to arrest him, the marshall said they would have to do it themselves. The Forest Service decided not to press charges.[2]

His patent was finally approved in 1926, but only after Harold Coolidge explained the situation to his cousin, the president.[3] By then, Hasselborg knew all too well why the Forest Service had given him such a hard time. Word was out in Juneau that a California company was about to sign a contract to log much of Admiralty Island. Lake Alexander would be dammed and water

Allen Hasselborg standing in the doorway of his cabin at Mole Harbor, c. 1939. *Courtesy of P. Sheppard*

sent down through a tunnel to a hydroelectric plant and pulp mill at Mole Harbor. Nobody had told Hasselborg when construction would begin, but it seemed like a sure thing.

Surprisingly, he had a mixed reaction to the news. In one letter to Flora, he sounded pleased that Mole Harbor was crawling with land speculators who said his homestead might be worth something someday.[4] A year later, however, he was having second thoughts. "I hope you can get to visit me some time before Admiralty is deforested," he told Dixon.

> The woods are full of [timber] cruisers and other experts and Mole Harbor is apt to be a hive of industry soon. Hasselborg Lake is supposed to swallow Beaver and Alexander and empty through

148

a tunnel into Mole Harbor at my place. I want to
be somewhere else when it happens.[5]

Writing his nephew Raymond, he made it clear that "somewhere else" was far from Alaska: "I moved 75 miles from town to
get away from too many (how do you spell NABORS) and now it
looks like they are going to build a big pulp mill on top of me. If
they do I will sell out and go to Mexico or China or somewheres."[6]
Although he knew he might have to leave Mole Harbor, he had
decided to wait and see what happened next.

Little did he know at the time that his fate had already caught
up with him: in the fall of 1926, John Holzworth had blown into
his life on a charter boat (Hasselborg called it a "booze" boat)
from Ketchikan.[7] When the New Yorker first showed up at Mole
Harbor, he had been trying to shoot a brown bear for two weeks.
Hasselborg took him out, and Holzworth made a fool of himself,
wounding one bear and letting a second one escape.[8]

Two years later, Holzworth visited again, this time with a
professional cameraman from Wrangell named Dick Surratt.[9]
Although Hasselborg spent almost a month with them photographing and filming bears, Holzworth was out of shape,
constantly complained about the weather, and was scared to go
into the woods alone. Surratt was a competent photographer, but
Holzworth exposed film when there wasn't enough light, rarely
used a tripod, and cleaned his lenses with a dirty handkerchief.
Nevertheless, at the end of their 1928 trip, Hasselborg agreed to
go out with him again. "Have just got back from a very good movie
hunting trip with a New Yorker who is a close personal friend
of Al Smith's and was acquainted with the [Woodrow] Wilsons
also," he wrote Flora soon after Holzworth left.[10] "I never vote
but if you cast a few for Al Smith you may get to visit me in the
Governors Mansion rent free and furnished, as this friend of Al

Smith's is quite a politician and has taken quite a fancy to me and my policies."[11]

By the next spring, Holzworth had written to say that he would be bringing along a college professor named William Cumming. When the two of them arrived in June, they were with Trevor Davis on Davis's boat; also aboard was Holzworth's dog, a terrier named Woof. Hasselborg led them on a month-long excursion up Seymour Canal, into the mountains west of Mole Harbor, and across Stephens Passage to Tracy Arm. He enjoyed visiting with his friend Davis and talking to Bill Cumming, who was eager to hear all about Admiralty Island, brown bears, and Hasselborg's life as an Alaskan homesteader. But Holzworth got on his nerves again, as did Woof. The little dog regularly "leaked" on the floor and was generally the "nastiest, dirtiest no good little brute" Hasselborg had ever seen.[12] When they finally left, Hasselborg hoped he'd seen the last of Holzworth for a while, but before long, he began wiring "like a lunatic,"[13] trying to set up a fall hunt with two New York bankers.

By the time he arrived in Juneau early in September, his entourage had grown to include two packers and a boatman, and he had appointed himself head guide. Though miffed by his sudden demotion, Hasselborg had a good time with the two bankers, who managed to shoot a small deer and a young brown bear. Holzworth, on the other hand, was so scatter-brained and full of himself, Hasselborg admitted that he was rather nasty to him before he left. By then, their relationship had definitely soured. "The big bum Holzworth had a Prof. of english with him this year and has 'wrote' a book to be called, 'My Friend the Bear'," he told Flora.

> It will be pretty good I believe and you may see
> my name in it. It was a very nasty wet year but he

got a lot of bear pictures again anyway. . . . He got two of the J. P. Morgan partners to come on a short hunt with me. It was a very poor hunt on account of the big bum's mismanagement, but I got on fine with the plutocrats, Ewing and H. P. Davison, and they want to come again and do it right.[14]

Four days after Hasselborg wrote that letter, a young Forest Service employee named Jack Thayer was killed by a bear on Admiralty Island. A gruesome mauling sensationalized in the press, it struck a raw nerve in Alaska. Ranchers in northwestern Alaska had long been complaining about bears attacking their livestock, and now, with Thayer's death, demands for more government control of brown bears gained enthusiastic support in Southeast. Juneau was outraged. Times had been hard recently. The big Alaska-Gastineau mine had shut down for good, only a few small pulp mills were still struggling to stay in operation, and a drastic decline in the salmon catch had forced several canneries to close. Many people in town were pinning their hopes on the Admiralty timber sale. Thayer had been a fine young man helping the Forest Service plan it. The bear had come after him unprovoked. "Exterminate Brown Bears!" screamed the headline of an editorial in a Juneau newspaper.

> The brown bears serve no good purpose. They are essentially killers. It is bad enough to have them destroy game animals and salmon. It is too much when they turn their attention to people upon whom we must depend for the development of Alaska.
>
> It may be that there are places in Alaska where bears ought to be protected, for the pleasure of

sportsmen. Whether this is so or not, southeast Alaska is not one of those places. We have too much to do to make room for settlers and industrial workers to permit this menace to hang over us. The bear ought to be exterminated—and the extermination work ought to begin at once.[15]

Although the Alaska Game Commission tempered its reaction with careful statements about the value of brown bears as big-game trophies, only two weeks after Thayer's death it announced a liberalization of Alaska's hunting laws. While emphasizing that Alaskans did not want to completely exterminate brown bears, the commission ruled that in order not to stand in the way of increasing industrial development, as of July 1, 1930, except in a few small areas, Alaskans could now hunt brown bears wherever and whenever they wished.[16] On Admiralty, Baranof, and Chichagof, the islands in the southeast region with the largest brown bear populations, the season would be open when the salmon were spawning and the bears were much more vulnerable than at any other time of the year.

Such vendettas against brown bears were nothing new to Alaska, where, in the long tradition of the American frontier, bears were seen as obstacles in the path of progress—with a unique Alaskan twist. As the historian Morgan Sherwood explains:

Periodically, Alaska civic leaders advocated the extermination of the animals and made Ursus the symbol of an alleged colonialism that was inspired by conservationist sentiment and directed by bureaucrats in Washington, D.C., working in concert with vested absentee interests, a colonialism that prevented resident Alaskan entrepreneurs from exploiting the territory's natural resources and prevented resident politicians from setting the terms of that exploitation. The bear question was effective bait to attract local support for home rule because it exposed elements of a class issue: the struggling but hardy, independent pioneer versus the effete eastern conservationist and wealthy sportsman with the power of big government in his hands.[17]

Just as Alaska's civic leaders must have expected, the Game Commission's liberalization of the hunting regulations soon caught the attention of conservationists and wealthy sportsmen in the states. By 1931, several dozen national conservation and sportsmen's organizations had endorsed what the beleaguered Forest Service had taken to calling the Save-the-Bear Campaign. Some of the most vocal support came from Arthur N. Pack and William Finley of the American Nature Association, an East Coast conservation organization, and Stewart Edward White, a well-known American writer of western novels. In the early 1930s, all three men came up to Admiralty Island to go camera hunting with Hasselborg. Writing in *Nature*, the American Nature Association's magazine, Pack made a point of describing Hasselborg talking bears out of charging, noting that the famous Alaska guide would rather watch bears than shoot them.[18] Finley and Pack's film, *The Great Bear of Alaska*, which featured many shots of Hasselborg, was effectively used to win broad support for the conservationists' cause.

In articles for *The Saturday Evening Post* and *American Forests*, Stewart White also scoffed at Alaskans' claims that brown bears were dangerous. He himself had been close to more than seventy bears while out with Allen Hasselborg, "the best-informed bear man in Alaska," he said, and had never been attacked.[19]

153

Allen Hasselborg, standing at camera, with visitor, photographing bears on Admiralty Island. *Courtesy of Oregon Historical Society*

Anyway, White argued, the Forest Service was wrong to promote timber development in southeast Alaska, as the depression had curtailed the nation's demand for pulpwood. Admiralty had a very small percentage of the commercially harvestable timber in southeast Alaska and, given the value of its other resources, particularly its bears, logging it just didn't make sense.

> In no other part of the world does this animal exist. Fortunately, he is at present rather numerous within his habitat. But inevitably the settlement and development of the country will result in his more or less gradual diminution, until at last he will persist, if persist he does, only in districts of the mainland so broken and remote that, as far

as the public is concerned, he might as well not exist.[20]

At the center of the storm of protest was none other than John Holzworth. As director of the New York Zoological Society's Alaska Bear Committee, he soon became a relentlessly loud, often irresponsible, gadfly who deluged elected officials with letters, convinced dozens of newspapers to run editorials, and encouraged thirty influential organizations to pass resolutions condemning Alaska's new regulations and boosting Admiralty Island as a sanctuary for bears. In nine talks broadcast over NBC radio and in impassioned testimony before the U.S. Senate Committee on Wildlife Resources, he frequently referred to Allen Hasselborg, "a self-educated scientist and intrepid hunter," who had introduced him to the bears of Alaska.[21]

In 1932, Holzworth wrote a long letter to a Juneau newspaper in which he extolled the virtues of Admiralty Island as a tourist destination and claimed that logging it would create only a hundred jobs, most of which would go to outsiders. The island was home to five thousand brown bears, he said, more than half of all the brown bears in Alaska. They were a valuable resource and not as dangerous as Alaskans said they were; Allen Hasselborg, an acknowledged expert on bears, could stop them just by yelling at them. In fact, Holzworth said, the doctor who bandaged Hasselborg after a bear mauled him had said it was his twenty-third bear case, and each time the bear had either been wounded or trying to escape. Thayer's death was certainly unfortunate, Holzworth was careful to add, but the young forester had made the fatal mistake of shooting at a bear with a .30/06 rifle—too light a caliber—and with the wrong kind of ammunition.[22]

Caught off guard by the Save-the-Bear Campaign, Alaskan officials and the Forest Service mounted a belated defense.

"Public in Alaska much incensed over situation and local feeling rapidly growing Forest Service and Biological Survey being dominated and dictated to by outside interests," Alaska Forest Service Commissioner Charles Flory wired an assistant early in 1932.[23] "If too many concessions made to propagandists, Alaska press and various organizations will enter the campaign, attack bureaus." *The Daily Alaska Empire* denounced eastern conservationists for their "emotional appeals" to "sentimentalists" and "nature lovers whose fears had been aroused by skillful dissemination of untruths and statements of half-facts."[24] The Forest Service argued that the Game Commission's new regulations did not threaten the future of Alaska brown bears, because they were already protected by sanctuaries amounting to an area almost as large as the state of New Jersey. And while the bears were certainly valuable as big game trophies, they should be controlled in areas where they might conflict with industrial development.[25] Although the bear "propagandists" were right in saying that Admiralty Island had a relatively small percentage of the commercial timber in the panhandle, it still had enough to create about a thousand new jobs; locking it up would eliminate a potential source of revenue to the government and be a serious blow to Alaska's pulp industry.[26]

Hasselborg may have first got wind of the Save-the-Bear Campaign in the fall of 1930, when Holzworth sent him an autographed copy of his book, *The Wild Grizzlies of Alaska*.[27] Dedicated to Allen Hasselborg, "Learned in the Lore of the North, Wise in his Judgment of Men and Animals, Sage in the Ways of the Bear," it described Holzworth's camera hunts on Admiralty, using many photographs and anecdotes about Hasselborg to argue against logging the island and in favor of increased protection for Alaska brown bears. Hasselborg was depicted as a wise, if eccentric, Alaskan homesteader and bear expert who had

Allen Hasselborg (left) and John Holzworth, Admiralty Island, 1928, from *The Wild Grizzlies of Alaska*. Hasselborg's note under this photo in his copy of the book stated: "Half way and the big bum half dead." *Photograph by D. Surratt. Courtesy of G.P. Putnam's Sons*

learned to get along with bears—living proof that bears were not dangerous brutes but interesting and valuable animals threatened by over-hunting and the greed of the timber industry.

By the time he had finished reading the first chapter, Hasselborg was furious. He had crossed out entire paragraphs, rewritten sentences, and filled the margins with corrections and angry exclamations: "rot," "imaginary," "fiction."[28] The book was "a lot of bunk, misinformation and lies," he told Flora. "Was thinking of suing him for libel for a while. Havent read only the first chapter and glanced through the rest."[29]

It was bad enough that Holzworth took credit for the book when Hasselborg knew it had been written by Cumming and that many of the photographs had been taken by Dick Surratt.[30] It was also embarrassing to be associated with so many misspellings of Alaska place names and mistakes in geography. Cumming had even said that the *Bulldogg* leaked and that Hasselborg was careless with camera equipment, which suggested that he was an incompetent guide.[31] But what really bothered him was that the book made him out to be a cranky, old misfit. In one passage, Cumming described him as an "Old Man" who had "developed an antipathy . . . against Civilization, Bureaucrats and Women."[32] When he read that, Hasselborg angrily crossed out "civilization" and "women."[33] He had been hoping to read about a likable expert on bears, a hard-working homesteader with a healthy disrespect for government, and instead found himself portrayed as an ill-mannered, eccentric, old misogynist. In an attempt to describe a colorful Alaska sourdough, Cumming had put Hasselborg's deepest insecurities about himself on display for the whole world to see.

People who visited Hasselborg in the 1930s remember that he was furious at Holzworth. "Holdsforth [referring to Holzworth] had been shell-shocked during the First World War," Hasselborg said, and had spent most of 1927 in a mental institution "for the good of the insides of his head."[34] Teddy Holdsworth, a sportsman from Boston who went hunting with Hasselborg in 1934, remembered being scared to tell Hasselborg his last name ("spelled with a 'd,'" he insisted—"no relation!"[35]) and how Hasselborg just grumbled and gave him a dirty look.

By then, a second book with Holzworth's name attached to it, *The Twin Grizzlies of Admiralty Island*, had further angered Hasselborg. Written for teenage boys, it told the story of two orphaned brown bear cubs taken in by an old naturalist named

Mr. Boston who lived at Mole Harbor with a terrier named Crab. Mr. Boston was a thinly disguised version of Hasselborg, the twin grizzlies were a lot like the cubs he had captured at Yakutat in 1908, and Crab sounded suspiciously like Woof, Holzworth's "miserable excuse for a dog."[36] Like *The Wild Grizzlies of Alaska*, the New Yorker's second book was "a badly mixed up lot of stuff," "the rankest kind of fake fiction," Hasselborg said.[37] "A most unnatural history of the brown bears, beavers and other Fauna and Flora of Admiralty Island," he wrote on the last page of the copy Arthur Pack sent him.[38] "This fool book must have been written by some ghost writer who knew less even than Holzworth of Admiralty Island and its wildlife."[39] Again he found himself described as an odd old man, though this time Holzworth or his ghost writer had gone even further. In a passage in which Mr. Boston remarked that female bears with cubs have more sense than most women, the narrator described Mr. Boston as "a women hater." "HOW COME?" Hasselborg wrote in large capital letters in the margin, deeply insulted.[40]

Almost as offensive was the book's portrayal of Mr. Boston as a nature-worshipping conservationist, "filled with a feeling of awe for the mysterious workings of the life force in every breathing thing."[41] Hasselborg was annoyed that such fuzzy, unscientific thinking had been attributed to him, and even more bothered by Mr. Boston's claim that the timber industry wanted to kill all the bears in southeast Alaska. "This fool rotten book was printed on pulp to make money by it," he wrote angrily in the margin.[42] As Mr. Boston continued to moralize against the timber industry's destruction of natural beauty, he became furious, firing "rot"[43] seven times onto the same page with a startling comment at the bottom: "Holzworth was paid by pulp interests to kill Alaska pulp business."[44] As a long-time Alaskan well aware that large corporations had often taken economic advantage of the territory, it was easy for him to subscribe to the rumor in Juneau that Holzworth had been hired by outside pulp companies intent on stifling competition from Alaska. Why else would a shady New York lawyer with friends in high places suddenly show up to block a project that promised to bring relief to Juneau's economy?[45]

In any case, Hasselborg certainly wasn't opposed to logging. In 1934, he told Dixon he was against turning over Admiralty to the bears. A gradual harvest of timber might even help the bears, he said, because logged areas produced more berries, and bears ate more berries than salmon.[46] And he vehemently disagreed with Holzworth's claim that the Admiralty bears were threatened by over-hunting, trigger-happy fishermen, and Forest Service employees. In 1932, he told a Juneau newspaper editor that the island's bear population had increased three hundred percent in the last twenty-five years, ever since the sale of brown bear skins and other body parts had been outlawed.[47] While he was worried that he might have to abandon his homestead, and no doubt pleased that the conservationists were giving the Forest Service such a hard time, he wasn't about to join them and make enemies of everyone in town. As for the bears, he had never thought much about wildlife conservation unless it affected him personally. During his years as a hunter, when he found areas where bears had been exterminated, he had been annoyed only because other hunters had gotten there first. He complained about poachers only when he thought he wasn't getting his fair share. In the early 1920s, when the government began offering a bounty on bald eagles, he shot dozens of them, saying that someone else would shoot them if he didn't.[48] Wildlife wasn't sacred to him by any means; it was there to be used. As long as he had enough for his own use, he didn't much care about anyone else.

160

Despite his sharp criticism of Holzworth and the Save-the-Bear Campaign and his statement to Dixon that a gradual timber harvest might help the bears, a question his sister Ebba asked him in 1932 suggests that he could not, or would not, make up his mind: "Please tell me," she pleaded, clearly exasperated, "do you or do you not want Admiralty Island made into a sanctuary for bears?"[49] He had long been cynical about politics, convinced that the government was controlled by millionaires and bureaucrats. Although he never hesitated to denounce government officials in Juneau when he thought he had been wronged, and had no compunctions about repelling the Forest Service with gunfire, the battle over Admiralty Island was a far more complicated situation. He was a loner, not given to working—or thinking—in a crowd. In the past, his political opinions had been private and personal, with no clear sense of any larger, social responsibility. He had run away from his family, fled Douglas Island to escape too many neighbors, and when faced with the possibility of a pulp mill at Mole Harbor, his first instinct had been to flee again, this time "to Mexico or China or somewheres."[50]

By the mid-1930s, the depression had killed the timber sale on Admiralty and the Save-the-Bear Campaign had forced major changes in Alaska's official policy toward bears. The Game Commission had established several new bear sanctuaries and hired more game wardens. In the Southeast region, hunters now had a shorter hunting season and a bag limit of one bear a year. The commission had also completed the first thorough survey of the bears on Admiralty and reported about a thousand animals holding their own.[51] Two new sanctuaries amounting to about five percent of the island would provide the bears with further protection while giving scientists and tourists more and better opportunities to observe and photograph them.

As a genuine Alaskan homesteader who had learned to get along with bears, Hasselborg had been a powerful symbol for the conservationists. Merely by associating him with their cause, they had succeeded in drawing much national attention to Admiralty Island for the first time. The Save-the-Bear Campaign had also forced Hasselborg to publicly divulge his knowledge of brown bears, thus further establishing his reputation as the best-informed bear man in Alaska. The Game Commission's estimate of a thousand bears on Admiralty came from several government employees who spent most of one summer walking almost every drainage on the island. Yet several years before the results of that survey were published, Hasselborg gave a newspaper reporter approximately the same figure.[52] It seems he wasn't boasting too much when he told a friend he had hiked and hunted every one of Admiralty's sixteen thousand square miles. "I knew every bear on some of these watersheds," he said, "and every one of those bears knew me, too."[53]

11

THE HERMIT OF

MOLE CREEK

IN THE EARLY 1930S, largely because of the Save-the-Bear Campaign, Hasselborg was more in demand as a guide than ever before. The depression also brought him more "parties," many of them wealthy businessmen from the states. "Hard times is always good times in the guiding business, as they want to get away from it all," he told his family.[1] "Ten days ago a yacht dropped into my harbor," he wrote Flora one spring. "It belonged to a little girl. I thought first that she was one of those movie queens and that her father who was along was an old hoosier, but it turned out he was worth 40 millions and had given her the yacht for a Christmas present."[2] The "little girl" must have caught Hasselborg's eye, for he had noticed that she didn't wear a wristwatch, "nor drink or smoke or even eat candy, and she wore her hair long."[3]

She had killed black bears and other game, but had failed to get grizzlies on two trips to B.C. [British Columbia] and wanted one more than

diamonds or pearls. The season is one month late
and we had to get out in the hills in the snow. It
was hard going and bears would have to be shot at
short range. After 4 days and pretty good chances
papa decided it was too rough and dangerous, so
we put in 3 days sightseeing and they left. . . . Her
yacht is chartered to "Kodak" Eastman for the
month of June, and I am to be with him. He is 76
years old and said to be a terrible old crank.[4]

George Eastman, the inventor of the Kodak camera, lived up
to his reputation during his hunt with Hasselborg the summer of
1930. He couldn't shoot straight without resting his rifle on
Hasselborg's shoulder and was so cranky Hasselborg wouldn't let
him land at Mole Harbor.[5] That may have been the beginning of
Hasselborg's falling out with Campbell Church, Jr., the charter
boat operator who had arranged Eastman's hunt. The following
year, Church hired him several more times, then in 1932 offered
him $2,000 to be what Hasselborg derisively described as "a wise
guy on a yacht."[6] By then, Hasselborg had had enough. "I am not
working for Church anymore," he told Flora in 1933. "I was so
sore at the whole outfit all last year that I wanted to bite myself
every time I happened to think about anything."[7] The next two
summers, he guided a few hunters and photographers who asked
him especially to take them out, but after 1935 he refused to buy
a guiding license. "Too much red tape and the charter yachts have
made a fool of the whole thing," he explained. "The cheap tinhorns
who pay $6000 for a trip now can't or don't kill their own bears
usually. The licensed guides out of Juneau are two barbers, two
carpenters, one cook, one sign painter, one drug clerk and one
halibut fisher. They never leave town except on these trips which
are their vacation."[8]

Although guiding had been a good way to make money, it had proved to be much more trouble than it was worth. He had moved out to Mole Harbor to get away from neighbors, but the Save-the-Bear Campaign and then the depression had brought a whirling circus of land speculators, bureaucrats, "conservation racketeers"[9] tourists, and "cheap tinhorn"[10] sportsmen crashing in on him anyway. "I have quit the guiding business," he told Flora in 1935.

> All I want is to be left alone to grub and dig to suit myself. My radio quit a few days ago. Don't know whether I will try to have it fixed, as the music is mostly very poor and the news is just the same old thing over and over all to prove that we are mostly fools and the rest crooks and rogues.[11]

In the late 1930s, after Stewart White gave him a more powerful radio, he could tune in stations as far away as Tokyo and Berlin.[12] To him, it sounded as if a worldwide revolution was just around the corner. Several millionaires he knew were now "ex-millionaires," he told Flora, and were talking about coming up to live with him when the revolution started.[13] "Most everything I hear makes me think this is a foolish world and getting more so all the time," he said.[14] "Don't worry about me. If all your civilization crumbles I will be able to get along quite well."[15]

Compared to other Americans, Alaskans generally got along quite well during the depression. A variety of New Deal programs and then, as the Second World War drew near, Alaska's strategic military position, gave the territory its first big economic boost since the mining boom at the turn of the century. As the capital, Juneau was first in line for much of the government bounty, which included a bridge to Douglas Island, harbor improvements, and, for the local mines, a hike in the price of gold. Between 1930 and

Allen Hasselborg (center), with two visitors, Admiralty Island, 1931.
Courtesy of F. Hibben

1940, while Alaska's population grew by about twenty percent, Juneau's almost doubled.

Despite Juneau's growth, virtually all the land surrounding it was still wilderness. Admiralty Island had only about three hundred and sixty year-round residents, most of whom were Tlingits living in Angoon, on the west side of the island. During the summer, fishermen and cannery workers swelled the population to about a thousand. Alaskans were in the first flush of their long love affair with airplanes, however, which made much of the territory far more accessible. Whereas before, the area around Mole Harbor had been a long boat ride from Juneau, and only those with strong legs and at least some knowledge of the country could get up to the lakes, now anyone with enough money could fly in to hunt, fish, and trap. The navy had even taken aerial photographs of the island, for the first time baring its interior to public view.[16]

Then the Save-the-Bear Campaign drew national attention to the island for the first time. Because Admiralty was almost all federal land, it was ripe for New Deal make-work programs. By the late 1930s, hundreds of Civilian Conservation Corps recruits were busy building tourist facilities up at the lakes. On a reconnaissance of Lake Alexander in 1937, Hasselborg counted twelve new cabins, sixteen skiffs, brick fireplaces along the shore, and a big tourist lodge he suspected had been built mainly for government officials. As far as he was concerned, all bureaucrats were "useless or worse"; the only reasons "town people" put up with them was "account of their salary, which is circulated."[17] "The worst was the Head Landscape Architect for the Nat. Park Service," he wrote Raymond Sheppard. "He had his assistant and he had the use of planes and govt. boats and what the final result will be I can't imagine."[18]

Allen Hasselborg (right) with visitor, Admiralty Island, 1931.
Courtesy of F. Hibben

"Alaska is just swarming with college W.P.A. boys," he complained to Flora another year. "They don't do any work but are out on all kind of fool jobs. None of them know anything about their job and admit it. I insult them all so they avoid me somewhat."[19] When one visiting bureaucrat referred to bear dung as "scat," Hasselborg called him a "scatologist."[20] "In my opinion Hasselborg is a 'bull' scatologist of the first water," the visitor huffed in an official report, "and his comments should have little weight or bearing on any matter."[21] Another time, a Civilian Conservation Corps employee stopped by to interview Hasselborg for an official survey of the number of bears that had been killed on Admiralty that year. "He was from the states and had never seen a bear and knew nothing about them," Hasselborg reported. "I told him to put me down for eighty."[22]

Much more annoying to Hasselborg than the visits of bureaucrats were the "foolish" new game laws they invented. "The people of the Fish and Wildlife Service are a lot of dumb fools," he groused at one point.

> None of them know their stuff except out of books written by others like themselves. And now they have opened the season on beaver everywhere except Admiralty where there are beaver. The whole idea of these regulations is to get them violated and holler for more appropriations, more authority, more personnel, more boats, more planes, more chance for graft.[23]

In past years, he had made as much as $600 on furs; now he felt lucky if he made anything at all. Some winters, the bureaucrats didn't allow any trapping, and when they did, the season sometimes lasted only about a month. "I was in town 3 weeks ago," he told Flora one spring,

> but couldent write any letters as I was having such a row with the govmt. They closed the trapping altogether last winter and when I got in found the beaver trapping had suddenly been opened and the month was more than half gone. A notice had been mailed me February 20 and they also had broadcast the news they said, about 30 seconds or so. Well I have got the 10 beavers allowed and am going in to tell them another chapter or so.[24]

Another year they revised the regulations right after he made his last fall trip into town. "Have some fur I can sell," he wrote a few months later, "but the dam burocrats say the rest is illegal. Cursed the office men out for $1^1/_2$ hours about it and gave all their office girls a good laugh. Told them I will see it thru to the Supreme Court if necessary."[25]

One imagines him in that office in Juneau, just in from a long skiff ride, in his long black slicker and black rubber boots, smelling of wood smoke. As he berates an embarrassed government employee, his words shoot out in a quick stream of precise, ironic questions, witty denunciations, and exaggerated threats, spiced with mild profanity. Others in the office watch and listen, amused, if a bit intimidated, by this thick-set, rough-looking man with a full beard and dark eyes, a sudden, wild visitation from the country. Hasselborg is steaming mad, but he's also enjoying their attention, playing to the crowd after many months alone at Mole Harbor.

He was in his sixties then, and according to reports he sent his family, his health was fine. "As to how old time is using me, will say whenever I get to town everyone is complimenting me on my general appearance," he told Flora in 1938.[26] "I have got over the bum foot you asked about once by doing nothing for it. Have paid doctor bill of $2.50 twice and dident take the advice or treatment either time. Have got half of the old teeth and don't expect to go to the dentist again."[27] He was still keeping up with all the work to be done around his place: felling trees and digging out stumps, chopping firewood, tending a big garden every summer, deer hunting in the fall, and snow shoeing for hours through the mountains almost every day during the winter checking his traps.

He had to admit to Flora, though, that his beard was showing a little gray and he wasn't as "full of pep"[28] as when he first came

Allen Hasselborg at his cabin, Mole Harbor, 1941. Note awkward way he carries his right arm, a result of the 1912 bear mauling. *Courtesy of Alaska Historical Library*

to Alaska. His rheumatism bothered him so much he had quit shaking hands with people "even if they try to," and at times the ranch almost got the best of him.[29] "I dident get to answer your letters the last two times I was to town," he wrote Flora one year, "and now you ask me to tell you everything. Well the last trip to town was one continuous struggle for 17 hours to get there so I was not feeling like writing. And now I am back home, and there is 160 [sic] acres of a farm to be cleared and cultivated, besides the cooking, dish washing, wood and water, laundry, ect., so I won't try to tell you all the details."[30]

Now that he had quit guiding hunters and photographers, his only income came from his trap lines and from selling vegetables to fishermen and to grocers in town. One year when he had a bumper crop of potatoes, he told Flora he sold fifteen hundred pounds, gave away two thousand pounds to Indians who stopped by, stored four hundred pounds in his root cellar, and still had to leave four hundred pounds in the ground "undug."[31] He never made much from his garden, however—no more than about a hundred dollars a summer. Too much depended on getting fishermen to take his produce into town, and when the fishing was good, they were too busy to help.

Added to his troubles in the late 1930s was a drop in the Mole Harbor deer population. "Alaska isn't as it used to be," he told his family one fall. No one he knew had killed a buck yet that year, he said.[32] Though the season had been open for more than a month, he had seen only two does with fawns. The bureaucrats were allowing too much deer hunting, he explained, and, as a result of the Save-the-Bear Campaign, were giving too much protection to the bears. He was sure bears were increasing on Admiralty and killing too many fawns and fur animals. "With more protection [the bears] have about exterminated the beaver and get a lot of mink," he said.[33] On one short walk around Mole Harbor, he had found the remains of nine fawns killed and eaten by bears.[34] One man who visited him about that time described him as "blood-thirsty" about the bears.[35] "They killed and ate four of my fawns this spring," he said, "and some stranger has been digging my potatoes. If I don't stop them, they'll kill every deer on the island. The government keeps shooting the deer and protecting the bears. I can't understand such stupidity."[36]

One would like to think that his threat to "stop" the bears was just brash talk. For years he had been saying he shot his last one in 1918, as if proud to have kicked a bad habit. Now, in the late 1930s, sure that bears were killing too many fawns and beaver, still seething from the insults of the Save-the-Bear Campaign, fed up with the swarms of bureaucrats hatched by the depression, he lashed out at a convenient target. It's hard to deny a series of startling entries in his 1938 journal, the first dated April 27, the last May 25, a total of eight entries clearly indicating that he shot eleven bears: "shotabear," "shotanotherbear," "shootingbears," "shotanubear," "8 shots 3 bears."[37] Maybe he just fired warning shots to chase them off, but "8 shots 3 bears" is too grimly conclusive, as if he was proud to have killed three of them so efficiently.

And then there's a story told by Stan Price, who at the time was living in Windham Bay, on the mainland, about twenty miles east of Mole Harbor. Price remembered a second time Hasselborg was mauled by a bear, "not the time back when he was hunting for the Biological Survey, [but] in '38 or '39, somewhere along there. . . . Hasselborg went up into the woods at Pleasant Bay. I don't know whether it was to satisfy a pelt or what, but he shot a bear and didn't knock him down."[38] The bear must have grabbed Hasselborg by the shoulder, Price said, since he had four or five "fearful wounds" in his back. It was a while before a fisherman found him on the beach and brought him over to Windham Bay,

DAY	DATE	THERM. 8 a.m.	WEATHER	5 APRIL GARDEN RECORD
	1	42	∧ S C	two ft. sno in parks, a sprinkle
	2	46	O C	
sun	3	42	+ C	afloat
	4		+ C	Juno
	5		∧ S	"
	6		+ ∧	Hoty
	7	42	+ S	Moll
	8	42	∧ C	
	9	44	∧ + C	a Bear, moskitos
	10	42	∧ + C	grubbing
	11	44	∧ + C	"
	12	42	+ C	" 2½ to date
	13	46	∧ O S ∧	" 3/4
	14	46	O + C	B Bumblebee, frost
	15	46	O + S	Dorn "
	16	46	O + C	wood "
sun	17	42	∧ C	rin.
	18	40	U S ∧	sno squalls
	19	42	+ C	gentung
	20	49	O C	"
	21	48	O C	"
	22	54	O C	3 swallows, gardening
	23	56	O ∧ C	garden
sun	24	54	O C	6 row spuds, pipits
	25	52	O C	radish, oil, from a bar
	26	56	O S ∧	peas, onions, a violet 1/4
	27	48	+ S SE	shot a bear
	28	46	∧ S X	hermits, warblers, osprey a bear 1/2
	29	48	+ S	blueberries in bloom summer
	30	50	+ ∧ C	crows, some sno on beach
				5 in price

Allen Hasselborg's weather journal, April 1939. Note entry for
April 27: "shotabear." *Courtesy of Alaska Historical Library*

where Price's wife Edna bandaged him up. The tides weren't right, so they had to wait two days for a mail boat to take him down to the hospital in Petersburg. Hasselborg was "wild" to get out of the hospital, Price remembered. "Maybe the reason was he had no money, you know, to keep him in town; more like the case that he didn't need much medical attention." Anyway, Hasselborg left Petersburg the next day on a mail boat headed for Admiralty and got off at Mel Starkenburg's fox farm in Gambier Bay. "Mel tried to get him to stay over," Price recalled, "but he was wanting to go right on home. He walked all the way back through the trail to Pleasant Lake and to his house—hell, you know, it must be twenty miles. I don't think he'd had any sleep since he'd had his back patched up."

Stan Price wasn't a man who told tall tales, and his first-person account is so rich in authentic details, it rings quite true. Several published descriptions of Hasselborg also mention that he was mauled a second time, and other Alaskans besides Price vaguely remember the same incident.[39] Yet whatever went on between Hasselborg and the bears in the late 1930s, it didn't last long. After the shootings recorded in his 1938 journal and the encounter at Pleasant Bay that same year or the next, apparently he called another truce. It had been a secret war—at least he never mentioned it to his family, probably because he had been breaking the law. Perhaps the best explanation for his secrecy, however, is offered by Sigurd Olson, a former Fish and Wildlife biologist from Juneau who knew Hasselborg in the 1950s:

> I never could understand Hasselborg as far as bears were concerned. I just never knew whether he was putting us on or whether the tales we heard were true. He was a person who told you just what he felt he wanted you to know at the moment, and

whether it was consistent with the past, or actions that came subsequently, was highly immaterial to him. For the moment, if he wanted you to think that he didn't shoot bears, why, he was done killing bears. He wasn't an out-and-out liar; that's just the way he was; he was an intensely independent person.[40]

Hasselborg's brief vendetta against the bears may also explain why he reluctantly came out of retirement to guide Frank Hibben on a bear hunt in the summer of 1941. Hibben, a well-known anthropologist and avid big game hunter, later wrote a story about that hunt entitled *Hasselborg's Hang-out*. Although inaccurate in some of its details and written in the melodramatic style of men's magazines, it is worth retelling, as it is by far the lengthiest, most complete account of Hasselborg guiding a trophy hunter.[41]

The story begins with Hibben and his wife Eleanor cautiously approaching Mole Harbor and feeling relieved when "the old man" greets them cordially. As Hibben and Hasselborg are getting ready to leave the cabin (Mrs. Hibben didn't join them on the hunt), Hasselborg confiscates Hibben's bed-roll and fishing gear and pours oatmeal flakes into their pockets for food. As they walk up along Mole River, he is carrying only a light wooden pack frame. Several thousand feet up in the mountains, near the headwaters of Mole River, they arrive at one of Hasselborg's trapping shelters. Before turning in for the night, Hasselborg spreads hot coals over the ground to dry it, then a layer of ferns for Hibben to sleep on, instructing him to cover himself with more ferns to stay warm. During the night, a male bear, upset by their intrusion into its territory, lurks for a while just outside the light from

Allen Hasselborg at lean-to in mountains of Admiralty Island, 1941.
Courtesy of F. Hibben

Allen Hasselborg with brown bear shot by Frank Hibben, Admiralty Island, 1941. *Courtesy of F. Hibben*

the fire, stamping its feet angrily. Hasselborg grabs a flaming stick from the fire and yelling "Scat! Get out, you!" chases it off.

The next day, they walk higher into the mountains. Hasselborg stops often to look through his telescope. He spots several bears, but they're either too small or their fur is ragged where they've been rubbing against trees. Finally he sees a big one in a blueberry patch on a ridge above them. "There's your bear," he says calmly. Frank Hibben stares up at it, awed by its size. "You'd better get to shootin'," Hasselborg mutters. "He's getting ready to charge. Aim for the shoulder. Don't wait till he turns straight toward us, and don't miss." With that, he raises his "rusty" old .38/40 to his shoulder. Hibben still hesitates. "Shoot!" Hasselborg exclaims. Hibben fires and the bear comes barreling down the mountain, spattering blood as it tumbles past them and collapses not far below. Both men are just picking themselves off the ground when it suddenly rears up on its hind legs. "Don't stand there gawking—Close your mouth and for God's sake shoot him again before we're both killed," Hasselborg says. Hibben finishes the bear off just as it begins to lurch towards them. "He's about a twelve-footer," Hasselborg says as they begin to skin it. "It's a good skin, too, if you want such things."

Hasselborg was sixty-three the year he guided that hunt. The following year, he ruptured himself upending logs onto stump piles for burning, and took to wearing a truss some of the time. "Other times [I] shove the old thing back in when it comes out," he told Flora. "Can play a tune with it if there is gas inside."[42] More isolated and alone than ever, he pretended not to care. "Some of the meanest Franconia girls used to address me as 'Your Royal Highness,' and now I am only an old curiosity known as the 'Hermit of Mole Creek' or the old crank who keeps the Mole Harbor graveyard, ect. Well never mind, when this foolish war is over I will be as well off as anyone I guess."[43]

In 1944, his heart acted up and he had to visit the hospital in Juneau. Now it was no longer just a matter of his rheumatism bothering him or a little more gray in his beard: that year he wrote a will for the first time. He wasn't about to let old age slow him down, though. One friend who hiked into the mountains with him when he was in his seventies, described him as "almost tireless."[44] "It was wonderful to watch Hasselborg travel in the woods and along the slippery gravel of the river bed," Ralph Young recalled.

> He seemed to glide rather than walk. . . . When we did stop for a brief rest on that day's journey up a wild river and through the virgin rain forest, the old man had the knack of relaxing completely, as a wild animal does. Though our resting periods were only of about ten minutes duration, Hasselborg would close his eyes and actually manage to nap a few minutes. When he awakened, he reminded me of a grizzly bear that has been suddenly disturbed when bedded down—instantly alert and loaded with energy.[45]

As always, Hasselborg continued to expend much of his bearish energy on feuds with the government. Alaska's population had more than doubled as a result of the Second World War, which for the increasingly solitary, disgruntled homesteader at Mole Harbor, only meant more bureaucrats to contend with. In 1946, they struck again with a law requiring all Alaskan landowners to register their property.[46] By the time Hasselborg saw the notice in the newspaper, the deadline was only three days off and he had to make a special trip into town. "Let them know that I was part Mohawk and might go on the warpath so they fixed it all up in a hurry," he told Flora. "The man in charge of treasurer office is a half Tlingit citizen. His brother is in territorial legislature so you may understand how I as a Mohawk stand with them. . . . Have patent to 135 acres with Cal Coolidge name on it. This new registration is so the local grafters can tax me."[47]

Though his feuds with the government were as fierce as ever, he was less skittish, more relaxed, when he was in town. He didn't mind talking to friends and admirers who stopped him in the street. A Juneau newpaper reporter who interviewed him in 1950 noticed that he had "a mellow gleam in once-hard eyes." Frank Hibben's *Hunting American Bears* had just gone on sale in Juneau, and the reporter wanted to know what he thought of it. "Because writers wrote such crazy stuff about me, I didn't give any interviews for 20 years and was pretty critical of the things I read about bears," Hasselborg replied. "But it doesn't matter any more. Anything goes. I'm just getting too old to be critical any more." He didn't like Hibben calling him "legendary," however. "This insinuates that I am dead," explained. "Although I am 75 I am very much alive!"[48]

Describing Hasselborg in the years after the war, one acquaintance, Jack O'Donnell, used the words "peculiar" and "woods-queer."[49] He recalled being anchored near Mole Harbor one moonlit night and hearing an outboard motor off in the distance. "That was unusual—in those days there was nobody around out there, especially so late at night."

> I heard the engine running and then it stopped. This happened several times, so finally I got up out of my bunk. I looked all around . . . no boat, no nothing. I thought, "that's funny," but I finally went back in and laid down. Then I thought I heard something bump my boat, so I got up again and quietly came up the ladder and looked out. Here

was Hasselborg in his skiff over to the boat looking to read the name on it. So I said, "Do you want
to come in, Mr. Hasselborg?" and he let out a grunt,
started his engine and away he went. He was
getting a little odd about then.[50]

Sigurd Olson remembered landing at Mole Harbor and
Hasselborg running down the beach waving a machete and
yelling loudly to scare him away.[51] Ralph Young had a similar
experience. Deer hunting at Mole Harbor one fall, he heard a sound
that stopped him dead in his tracks and raised the hairs on the
back of his neck. "It was an ominous, chilling, moaning growl,"
Young recalled. "It was a sound I had heard before. I was sure
that directly ahead of me in the thick brush there was a wounded
grizzly bear that might attack at any moment." Rifle at the ready,
he backed slowly out of the woods. A few minutes later Hasselborg
appeared on the beach ahead of him. "He was heavily bearded,
walked with an inimitable style, and carried no rifle." He
demanded to know what Young was doing on his property. Young
said he was deer hunting. "There aren't any deer back there,"
Hasselborg replied "They're all over on the other side of the bay.
You should have come up and talked to me first. I'd have told you
where to hunt." Young thanked him for the offer, then mentioned
the wounded bear he'd just heard. Hasselborg looked at him
sharply. "How do you know there's a wounded bear in these
woods?" he asked. Young assured him that he knew what a
wounded bear sounded like. Hasselborg asked him again if he
was sure. Again Young confirmed what he'd heard. "Well, that
wasn't no wounded bear you heard back there," Hasselborg said.
"That was me." Young was dumbfounded: "The growling and
moaning couldn't have been more realistic had it been made by a

bear. It was the first time I had heard Allen Hasselborg talk like a grizzly bear."[52]

By then, Hasselborg wasn't going into town after September. The long, cold skiff rides made him "wobbly," he said,[53] and his outboard often broke down along the way. Karl Lane remembered seeing him adrift off Glass Peninsula, beating angrily on his engine with a wrench.[54] Once, it quit just south of Mole Harbor, and he had to be towed back home by a fishing boat. For four days he tried to fix it, then gave up and rowed all the way in, covering the seventy-mile distance in less than a week. On another trip, he ran out of gas thirty miles outside of town and had to row in again. He seemed in less of a hurry now, sometimes staying for as much as a month, occasionally even taking a room at a hotel. He wasn't ready to admit how hard it was getting to face the long, cold boat ride home. Now, besides the government, he was blaming his troubles on the weather. Though he had been complaining about it for years, always before he had been quick to defend it whenever his family said the weather below was better. He had kept daily records, been interested, even amused by it as long as it occasionally showed signs of improving. Now he was sure it had taken a permanent turn for the worse. In 1951 he told his family he had been able to shoot only one buck the previous fall because a heavy snowfall and cold weather had killed off the deer.[55] But his lack of success hunting was the government's fault, too. When he first came up to Alaska, he told Flora, "before there was any law," he could shoot ten or fifteen deer every year.[56] Now, he could shoot only one or two and had to save every scrap for canning, "even skin the legs to the hoofs and the head to the nose end and cook all the bones 10 or 12 hours for stock."[57] He might even have to sell his place, he said, and move to Florida.

Allen Hasselborg's cabin, Mole Harbor, winter of 1933.
Courtesy of P. Sheppard

Florida: a northerner's dream, his father's dream of paradise. He had been thinking about it at least since 1945, when he said that if he ever went south again he would want to settle "back in the mountains or swamps where the autos can't come."[58] It wasn't until 1949, however, that he decided to advertise his homestead as a "beaver farm" with an annual income of two thousand dollars.[59] Though the news that Old Man Hasselborg was selling his place caused something of a stir in town, nobody rushed to buy it. "Well, there was no sale and won't be neither I guess," he told Flora that fall, "as it was the worst spring and summer ever known and our climate has sure got a black eye."[60] "Now I am stuck here for life," he wrote the following year. "Could have sold out years ago. But now politics and changed weather have given Alaska such a reputation that it is no good for anyone but bureaucrats."[61]

184

The winter of 1950, Mole River froze to the bottom. It was still iced over in April when he started into town, and he had to drag his sled out half a mile to get to his boat. That fall, for the third year in a row, he was able to shoot only one buck. The next two winters were even worse than the winter of 1918: four feet of snow by Christmas and about that much still on his garden in April. He tried to trap, but both winters the bureaucrats cut the seasons too short, and fur prices were the lowest he'd seen in years. "Don't expect to sell the place, as it has no paved highway to town," he wrote Flora morosely in the spring of 1951. "Juneau has 25 miles of smooth paved roads out of town all lined with homes of bureaucrats and business people who live off of them."[62] None of the bureaucrats wanted to live so far from town, he explained, but he wasn't about to abandon thirty-six years of hard work.

In 1952, in a letter full of vague, distracted thoughts, he admitted to Flora that his mind wasn't what it used to be: "Well it will be a big job but I must answer your last few letters. I just can't write: partly account of hand, arm and shoulder and also the inside of my head."[63] He told a friend in Juneau that bears were coming too close to his cabin and he was sure they were coming to take him away.[64] "He was slipping away mentally toward the end," Karl Lane remembered.[65]

> He was a sharp guy, no question about that, he was as sharp as a razor. But he started to get all kinds of goofy ideas. The last time I saw him was in the spring when I took a hunter in there. He said, "Well, I went down to Florida this winter." And we said, "How did you go down?" And he said, "Well, I stowed on an Alaska steamer and got down to Seattle and then I hitchhiked across the country." But he hadn't left the country. I *knew* he

hadn't made that trip. It was all in his head. But we didn't say anything. Hasselborg just stared out the window. After a few minutes he said, "Well, I'm not really sure I made that trip down there. I might have been upstairs dreaming."[66]

Finally, in the fall of 1953, a building contractor from Georgia named H. G. Smith bought the homestead for $3,500.[67] Smith had come up to Alaska several times to hunt bears and had visited Hasselborg. According to one report, they hit it off so well, Hasselborg let him shoot a bear from the window of the cabin at Mole Harbor.[68] Though he now owned the homestead, Smith graciously offered to let Hasselborg stay there as long as he liked. An article in a Juneau newspaper described Mole Harbor as "a wrestling ground for some of the largest brown bears in the world," suggesting that Hasselborg's bears might soon be more available to hunters.[69] "Although Hasselborg never ceases cursing the big brownies as nuisances, he is quick to chase off any hunter who sets foot on his domain," the article said.[70]

Hasselborg stayed through one last winter and didn't go into town until the first week in May when he shipped several hundred pounds of books, clothes, and camping gear down to a nephew in Florida. On May 24, 1954, he made his last trip to town. His plans were vague: he would visit Ebba in Washington, then go down to look for land back in the Big Cypress Swamp, where he could shoot deer and turkey and grow a garden. He would say later than his trip by taxi to the Juneau airport June 8 was the first time he had ridden in a "hellcart."[71] Soon after the plane took off, word went around the cabin that Old Man Hasselborg was aboard, so the pilot made a detour down Seymour Canal and flew low over Mole Harbor. Everyone looked for the new owner, but he didn't seem to be around. Hasselborg said Smith was probably out bear hunting.[72]

12

OLD SOURDOUGH

FOR MORE THAN HALF a century Hasselborg had lived mostly alone in the peace and stillness of the Alaska wilds. All that time he had never been below and had left southeastern Alaska only once. For thirty years he had gone no farther from Mole Harbor than the seventy miles into town. Gradually his territory had become smaller, from his first rambling hunts for Annie Alexander and C. H. Merriam, to an occasional excursion off Admiralty as a guide in the 1930s, to the last fifteen years, when Mole Harbor nearly became his whole world.

Now, in an airplane for the first time in his life, high over Admiralty Island, he could have dropped down almost anywhere and known just where he was—by a pond where he had trapped beaver, on a ridge where he had picked blueberries, in a meadow he knew would be bright with wildflowers in another month or so. What were his thoughts as the plane passed low over Mole Harbor and he looked down on his small clearing and the beaches he had walked so often in tune with the tides? Was he reminded of a day long ago when he rode in a wagon past the burnt-out remains of his family's house in Franconia, then as now bound for

Allen Hasselborg with three of his sisters at Flora Hasselborg Merritt's house in Biloxi, Mississippi, 1954. Left to right: Allen, Nellie, Ebba, and Flora. *Courtesy of Sitka Pioneers' Home*

a new life in "the sunny south?" There *would* be something almost childlike about him in the months ahead as he wandered back to his family. To his sisters, Ebba and Flora, he would be the same as ever—their amusing, bull-headed, unpredictable, annoying Bro Allen. To everyone else he would be a colorful old Alaska sourdough looking for a place in the sun.

He spent the first night of his trip in Seattle and flew east the next day, arriving at Ebba's apartment in Washington, D.C., at about seven in the evening. It was so strange the way he suddenly appeared, Ebba would say later—so similar to a dream she'd had recently. She was sitting by a window reading her mail when she happened to look out and see a taxi pull up to the curb. When she opened the front door, Allen was just getting out of the cab. "Here she is now!" she heard him say to the dazed-looking driver. Though the temperature was in the nineties, he was wearing a red and black flannel shirt, an ancient corduroy jacket, a pair of pants he had bought more than forty years ago, some heavy leather boots Ebba's son Raymond had left at Mole Harbor in 1933, and a bowler hat he had acquired in Douglas at the turn of the century. His only luggage was a small, battered, black satchel.[1]

For the next few days, he kept talking as if he were still in Alaska and seemed to get a kick out of occasionally forgetting where he was, or even who Ebba was. Spotting himself in a full-length mirror for the first time, he was shocked that he looked so humpbacked. Ebba told Flora that Allen looked and acted at least ten years older than he was and often forgot what she told him. Though he was generally well-behaved, he didn't like being fussed over; when she tried to iron his shirt, he groaned at her like a bear.[2]

Right away, he wanted to walk all over town, though he tired quickly and often had to sit down to rest. He couldn't figure out what was wrong with him. At first he thought the pavement was hurting his feet; then he decided "hellcarts" were to blame. He had suspected as much when he got his first whiff of the air in Seattle: everyone below was dying of carbon monoxide poisoning. "They can call this civilization if they want to, but I call it insanity!" he told Ebba after one particularly harrowing expedition through the streets of Washington.[3]

By then, even Hasselborg agreed that his coat and trousers were too old and dirty and that he needed shoes that weren't so heavy and hot. At a nearby Goodwill store, with Ebba's help, he bought a light summer suit and a short-sleeved white shirt. One of his nieces, Elinor Gardner, then took him to Sears. "He was immediately suspicious of the escalator," Mrs. Gardner recalled.

"He eyed it and eyed it, and then he hopped on it like a monkey and rode it up and down a few times. After a while it was no problem for him, with all the time he had spent on boats."[4] Up in the men's department, he caused quite a stir. Proudly displaying his old bowler hat, he offered to trade it for a new one; Sears would do well on the exchange, he said, as his hat had appeared in many newspaper photographs and was quite famous in Alaska. Although Mrs. Gardner urged him to buy a lighter hat, he said he didn't need one and, on second thought, he didn't need a new hat at all—his old bowler would do just fine. With a wad of bills he pulled from a shirt pocket, he paid for three pairs of lightweight long underwear, a pair of BVD's, three pairs of socks, and a windbreaker. When the zipper on his new windbreaker gave him trouble, he explained to the crowd of onlookers that he didn't know anything about zippers since they weren't much use in southeastern Alaska, what with all the wet weather up there.[5]

With a pair of white tennis sneakers donated by his old friend Harold Coolidge, his new outfit was complete. After touring Mount Vernon and the National Zoo with the Gardner family, he went to the Smithsonian to visit the director of the National Museum of Natural History. He was a hit, entertaining the director and his staff with hunting stories and descriptions of Alaska as he examined bear skins and skulls he had collected for Dr. Merriam.

By the end of July, however, his welcome at Ebba's was beginning to wear thin. It wasn't just his absent-mindedness and odd opinions about everything, Ebba told Flora; it was that he seemed so attached to her, which made her uncomfortable. "I didn't know he regarded me so highly," she confided, "but I'll tell you I surely think he has a mother complex and I think he has got me mixed up with her somehow."[6] She assumed he would be leaving soon for Florida, as he said he had already sent some clothes, books, and a tent down to their nephew, Jack Merritt, in Clewiston. Lately,

Allen Hasselborg with his great nephew, Bruce Gardner, visiting Mount Vernon, Virginia, 1954. *Courtesy of E. Gardner*

Allen Hasselborg at Flora Hasselborg
Merritt's house in Biloxi, Mississippi,
1954. *Courtesy of E. Gardner*

though, he had been talking about going back to Alaska; the
man who bought his homestead had said he would always be
welcome there, so he was thinking about trapping on Admiralty
that winter.

Ebba wasn't surprised when that turned out to be just
another vague fantasy. By the end of July, she had put him on
a train to Florida. He stayed with Jack Merritt and his family
until September, then went up to Biloxi, Mississippi, to visit
Flora. By October, he had bought an old twenty-three-foot cabin
cruiser, renamed her the *Ebba*, and set out on a seven-hundred-
mile voyage to Sanibel, an island off the coast of Florida where
Ebba owned property.

The first day he made it seventy-five miles down the coast to
Mobile, Alabama. The next day his engine quit in Bon Secour

Allen Hasselborg, Biloxi, Mississippi, 1955, aboard the *Ebba. Courtesy of Sitka Pioneers' Home*

Bay, the first of several breakdowns he would have along the way. "Broke down Bone Sucker Bay," he wrote cheerfully on a postcard to Flora. "At anchor rough water 3 days. Got tow to Wrecks Bay by yacht. Got repairs 12th [October]. Will be starting east 14th? Candy about all gone."[7] A week later, he was in St. Andrew Bay. The old Hasselborg house had long since burned down, he was told, though the homestead was still owned by Minnesotans. Hearing that one of the Hasselborgs had come in on a boat, a local newspaper sent a reporter down to the harbor to talk to him. In the paper the next day, he was described as "a real Alaska sourdough who had had enough ice and snow" and was "on the prowl for a small patch of Florida real estate."[8]

Civilization-Shy Alaskan Guide Docks At Holmes Beach, Muses On Career

By BOB HANSCOM

HOLMES BEACH — A grizzled, 79-year-old Alaskan sourdough who has used a telephone only once in 60 years, has ridden only once in an auto and hasn't eaten in a restaurant in 38 years visited Holmes Beach Yacht Club over the weekend in his 24-foot cruiser, the Ebba.

"The last time I used a telephone was 60 years ago when I talked to two women and pretty near got myself in trouble," he said.

"I haven't used one since and I'm not starting now. Tell that fellow if he wants to talk to me he'll have to come out here," Al Hasselborg told the manager of the club when an interview was requested.

FROM BILOXI

Hasselborg arrived after a month's boat trip from Biloxi, Miss.

After 52 years as a guide and trapper, Hasselborg left Alaska last June. His "shack" was in the wilderness 70 miles from Juneau or his closest neighbor.

During his years as a guide for bear hunting trips he said many famous people were in his parties: George Eastman, the camera magnate; Max Fleischmann, of the yeast company; Amos Berg, photographer for National Geographic Magazine; Arthur Pack, publisher of Nature Magazine; John M. Hollsworth, who wrote bear stories, and Harry P. Davidson and

(Continued on Page 26)

Al Hasselborg slowly guides his 24-foot cruiser, Ebba, into the channel at the Holmes Beach Yacht Club Basin, as he anxiously watches for obstructions. The hat Al is wearing was purchased in Alaska when he was courting in 1903. He remained a bachelor.

Alaskan Guide Recalls Past

(Continued from Page 25)

Buck Ewing, banking partners of J. P. Morgan.

SHUNS RESTAURANTS

Al hasn't eaten in a restaurant since 1916, and vows he never will.

Al was born Nov. 18, 1875, in Minnesota, 75 miles north of Minneapolis in a town called Fraconia, that he calls Plugtown — now a ghost town. He quit school at 15 when the teachers tried to make him study algebra and civil government.

He went to work in a logging camp and when he was 17, he moved with his family to St. Andrews Bay, Fla., now Panama City.

"The folks couldn't read or write back in those days," he said.

"There was one fellow up there in St. Andrews Bay who wanted to go to the state legislature, so he came to my sister and she taught him to read and write."

"WAS SHANGHAIED"

After spending five years as a fisherman, he started for Alaska by way of San Francisco. He shipped on the Arago, the oldest cod fishing boat on the Pacific coast.

He said there were 12 fishermen on the boat and all were shanghaied except himself. They spent seven months in Alaska waters fishing and each received $70 at the end of the trip, he said.

He sold his shack last June and booked plane passage to Washington, D.C., to see a sister who is

Florida newspaper article, November 1955.

Three hundred miles more, and he was tied up at a yacht club south of St. Petersburg. When a local newspaper reporter called asking for an interview, Hasselborg told the manager of the club that he wasn't about to use a telephone—the reporter would have to come down to the dock if he wanted to talk. "Civilization-Shy Alaskan Guide Docks at Holmes Beach, Muses on Career," read the headline in the paper. "The last time I used a telephone was 60 years ago when I talked to two women and pretty near got myself in trouble," he was quoted as saying. "I haven't used one since and I'm not starting to now." The old sourdough was bound for Sanibel Island, where he planned to live with his sister for the rest of his life, the article explained. He said he guessed he was "good for one or two more years."[9]

Almost two months after leaving Biloxi, he reached Sanibel. Ebba was pleased to see that he wasn't so pink and white any more and that he looked fit, though he had been living almost entirely on cocoa, oranges, whole-wheat bread, and candy. She also noticed that he had lost some of his social peculiarities, although he still insisted on wearing his rubber boots all day in the hot sun. It seemed a miracle that he had survived; even with all the right marine charts he had hit a reef north of St. Petersburg, luckily escaping unharmed.[10]

Before long, however, he began complaining that Sanibel Island was a mangrove swamp where nothing would grow. Ebba's land was so flat it made him nervous, he said; at high tide it was only a few inches above the sea. He had found a few raccoon tracks, but hadn't seen any wildlife—not even a squirrel—since he left Washington. And there were too many cars on the island and no place to keep his boat. Ebba tried to win him over. Her neighbors were friendly, she assured him, and she knew several houses where he could live rent-free, maybe even grow a garden, in exchange for taking care of the owners' boats. He wasn't interested. He wanted to live by a creek, he said.[11]

It didn't take him long to make up his mind. "Well I know I have had too much of the 'Sunshine State' and will have to go north again," he wrote Flora. "It gets *cold* at night sometimes, but up to 80 or more every day. . . . Cant locate on saltwater account of the mangrove. . . . People fishing everywhere. Saw one little snapper caught at the waterfront in two months. . . . If I sell the boat will go back to Alaska where there is a fine big pioneer home."[12]

A month later, he was even more determined to leave: "Well it will soon be time for me to start for . . . Alaska. It gets worse here, sunshine all the time, no wind and up over 80 every day. . . . This would be a pretty nice place for anyone who could stand the sunshine and use a car. No fish to be had except catfish near the sewer outlets. 86 in the shade today and 96 in the boat. I sweat and suffer and it is hard to write."[13]

By May, he had made the long journey back to Mississippi in the *Ebba* and was writing Leslie Yaw, the superintendent of the Sitka Pioneers' Home in Alaska, wanting to know how to apply for a "bearth."[14] In a few quick sentences, he summed up his life as an Alaska pioneer, then explained that he had gone down to Florida to live as a gardener. "Got small boat at Biloxi and cruised to the everglades and back. No place fit for boat and garden for sale and I cant stand the heat and sunshine. Will be able to pay my own fare when boat is sold. Haven't heard any news of Alaska for a year but you can learn from oldtimers of Juneau who I am."[15]

Three friends in Juneau—Trevor Davis, Volta Williams, and Edward Keithahn—sent glowing letters of recommendation to the Pioneers' Home, though Keithahn worried that Hasselborg might not fit in. "I have known Mr. Hasselborg for many years and know him to be a man of good character and moral habits and a truly worthy pioneer," Keithahn wrote.

> I have some doubts that he will be happy there, as he has lived alone for many years and might have some trouble making the adjustment, but he is surely entitled to have a chance at it. I have noticed that in the past several years he has mellowed considerably from his somewhat cantankerous past. But one thing I did discover about him: he likes to be lionized and made over.[16]

Having sold the *Ebba* at a loss, Hasselborg informed Yaw that he would be leaving for Alaska in a few days. "The Minnesota

Biloxi Miss. May 21 1955

MAY 13 1983

Pioneers Home. Sitka. Alaska.

Dear Supt, I am wanting to get a berth in your home, and dont know how to apply. Was born in Minn. 1875 sailed on Sch. Arago oct 1898 of Frisco for a 7 month codfish trip to Shumagin isles. Winter 1900-1901 was bulldozer in Treadwell mine. 1902 after my last trip below fished on Taku and chopped wood at Haines, clearing the fort site all winter 1903 worked at Rodman Bay mine and built a dory in Sitka pulled to Juneau Nov - Jan 1904 by way of Warms springs, Murder Cove and Oliver inlet. 1904-1905 prospected hunted bear and trapped. 1906 Trapped and trolled salmon at Pleasant bay 1907 began as guide and hunter for Alexander expeditions of U of Calif. for 3 years. Dixon Ent to Kenia. Was trapper and guide since, resigned as guide 1936. Last June started for Florida thinking I could live as gardner. got small boat at Biloxi and cruised to the everglades and back, no place fit for boat and garden for sale and I cant stand the heat and sunshine will be able to pay my own fare when boat is sold Havent heard any news of Alaska for a year but you can learn from oldtimers of Juneau who I am. Please let me know how to apply for berth.

Yours Truly

Allen Hasselborg

Biloxi Miss.

Formerly of Juneau since 1902

Allen Hasselborg's letter of application to the Sitka Pioneers' Home, May 21, 1955. "Can't stand the heat and sunshine . . . " *Courtesy of Sitka Pioneers' Home*

197

Sitka Pioneers' Home, Sitka, Alaska, 1983. *Photograph by J. Howe*

trip is off as all the oldtimers have died lately," he explained.[17] He flew from New Orleans on the Fourth of July and landed in Juneau the next day. On July 7, 1955, he was admitted to the Sitka Pioneers' Home. "The home is quite a place," he wrote Flora a few weeks later.

> I have a good room to myself. We get too much grub and bed with sheets washed weekly and free laundry. There is about 40 oldtimers in the hospital waiting to die. Not many arguments as we all know it all.[18]

He sounded content, if a little bored. The library at the home didn't have any books that interested him, so he often went down to the harbor to chat with fishermen. By November, he had a roommate, a Norwegian from Minnesota, and had also discovered a few old-timers he could talk to, one of whom he remembered from "the Klondike days."[19] Another pleasant surprise was a "fine looking big lady" who dropped in on him unexpectedly and turned out to be a distant relative from the Ballard side of the family.[20] She had since taken to inviting him out for Sunday lunch with her family, which he always enjoyed.

By January, he was already looking forward to another Alaska spring, though by then he knew he was dying of cancer. He told his friend Tom Park about that time that he expected to be gone in a month or two.[21] Writing letters, he could scrawl only one sentence at a time, pausing in between to rest. He couldn't remember words and was forgetting how to spell. "He was resigned to his fate," Yaw recalled. "He accepted it like a gentleman."[22] Talking with a friend, he said his only fear was that they might take him to his grave in a "hellcart" and ruin his afterlife.[23]

He was admitted to the hospital on January 19, 1956, and died four days later, at the age of seventy-nine. No member of his immediate family attended the funeral; pallbearers had to be hired for the ceremony. They drove him to the graveyard in a "hellcart" borrowed by the Pioneers' Home for such occasions—one of Sitka's fire trucks.

EPILOGUE

IF YOU WALK UP through a small grove
of trees in the Sitka graveyard, past fancy monuments to the
town's more prominent former residents, you will come to a
gently sloping hillside inlaid with rows of small, flat grave-
stones. Many are overgrown by grass and too weathered to read,
but if you look hard you'll find one with Hasselborg's name on it
and know that beneath it lie his bones.

While his homestead at Mole Harbor is still privately owned,
the land for many miles around it—about ninety percent of
Admiralty Island—is now within The Admiralty Island National
Monument. President Jimmy Carter established the monument
in 1978, ending a long, intermittent political battle that began
with the Save-the-Bear Campaign in the 1930s. Congress has since
added it to the National Wilderness Preservation System. As the
bear man who instructed and inspired the leaders of the campaign, Hasselborg thus played an important early role, however
unwittingly, in the preservation of more than 900,000 acres of
Alaska wilderness.

Although many current residents of Juneau have visited or
at least heard of Hasselborg Lake and Hasselborg River, few

Allen Hasselborg's cabin, Mole Harbor, 1982. Looking up Mole River.
Photograph by J. Howe

know anything about the man for whom they were named. As the government agency charged with managing Admiralty Island the U.S. Forest Service is at least partly to blame for that. Its feud with Hasselborg festered long after he died. In the 1960s, a group of zealous Forest Service employees in Juneau tried to rename Hasselborg Lake, and even began labeling it Admiralty Lake on official maps, before some of Hasselborg's friends protested and talked them out of it.[1] As recently as 1981, an official history of the Forest Service in Alaska dismissed him as "a squatter" who "cultivated the looks and style of a backwoods sage."[2] His cabin, arguably one of the most historic buildings on the island, was neglected for many years and collapsed to the ground late in the fall of 1983.

Somewhere between 1,600 and 2,000 brown bears live on Admiralty Island now, considerably more than the number estimated by the government in the 1930s. Until the mid-1970s, hunters shot about thirty every year. Since then, the average annual take has almost doubled. In 1984, aware of that increase and the growing number of tourists visiting the Pack Creek Sanctuary, the State Board of Game expanded the area of Seymour Canal closed to bear hunting. Besides Pack Creek and much of Seymour Canal to the south, the new Upper Seymour Canal Closed Area includes the Swan Creek drainage, where Hasselborg often took photographers. It doesn't include Mole Harbor.

Still, if you visit Mole Harbor at the right time of the year, you might see a bear nosing along the banks of Mole River, though odds are long that it will be a descendant of one of Hasselborg's bears. After he left for Florida, local hunters had a field day at Mole Harbor. "First Jack came out, he had to have his bear, and he shot one," Stan Price told me. "Then Smitty he had to have his bear and he shot one, and Mark had to have his and he shot one, and the next that came out was Doc Rude, and he shot a bear, too. Then they got hunters out there in the fall for $1,500 each. In two years' time they killed all the bear in that area big enough to shoot."[3]

Out where Mole River empties into the bay, you'll come upon the weathered bow section of the *Bulldogg* standing upright in tall grass, used now for storage by the homestead's owners. Near the site of one of Hasselborg's gardens, they have built a small

Seymour Canal, looking south from Swan Cove, 1984. *Photograph by J. Howe*

house and A-frame. Continue around the first bend in the river, and you'll find the remains of his cabin, a pile of rotten lumber in a tangle of young spruce and salmonberry. Ashes to ashes, dust to dust. You won't find Hasselborg's spirit there, but keep walking up Mole River half a day, bushwhack high into the mountains, and when you're well above the tree line, stop and look, and listen. Maybe you'll see it then and hear it in the silence that enfolds you.

NOTES

IN CITING WORKS in the notes, short titles have been used. Titles of collections and personal names have been identified by the following abbreviations:

AH	Allen Hasselborg
AH Papers	Allen Hasselborg Papers, Alaska Historical Library
FHM	Flora Hasselborg Merritt
GFC	Gardner family collection
JG Papers	Joseph Grinnell Papers
MH	Mary Hasselborg
RS	Raymond Sheppard
SFC	Sheppard family collection
UCMVZ	University of California Museum of Vertebrate Zoology

Introduction

1. Turner, "The Significance of the Frontier in American History."
2. Young, *My Lost Wilderness*, 120.
3. Shepard and Sanders, *The Sacred Paw*, xi.

4. Ibid., 72.

5. Thornton, "Subsistence Use of Brown Bear in Southeast Alaska," 53–54.

6. Jonaitis, *Art of the Northern Tlingit*, 81; Kamenskii, *Tlingit Indians of Alaska*, 74; Emmons, *The Tlingit Indians*, 132–133.

7. Kamenskii, *Tlingit Indians of Alaska*, 73; Holzworth, *Wild Grizzlies of Alaska*, 19–20.

8. Dixon to AH, 2 December 1944, AH Papers.

9. AH to FHM, 19 October 1931, GFC.

10. C. Davis, interview with author, 2 March 1981.

11. AH to FHM, 8 April 1951, GFC.

Chapter 1: Hasselborg's Domain

1. F. Hibben, "Hasselborg's Hang-out," in *Hunting American Bears*, 150.

2. Ibid.

3. Ibid., 151.

4. AH, from notes in his personal copy of Holzworth, *Wild Grizzlies*, 4, 11.

5. F. Hibben, "Hasselborg's Hang-out," in *Hunting American Bears*, 151.

6. Burg, "Fortress of the Bears," in *Alaska Fish Tales and Game Trails*, 26.

7. E. Hibben to author, 14 April 1982.

8. Young, *My Lost Wilderness*, 117–118. Other sources used to describe the interior of Allen Hasselborg's cabin include: the author's examination of its remains in the early 1980s; Davis, interview with author, 27 March 1982; Burg, "Fortress of the Bears," in *Alaska Fish Tales and Game Trails*, 26; Holzworth, *Wild Grizzlies*, 11; F. Hibben, "Hasselborg's Hang-out," in *Hunting American Bears*, 151; and AH, from notes in his copy of Holzworth, *Wild Grizzlies*, 11.

9. Price, interview with author, 14 March 1981.

10. Cahalane to author, 31 August 1982.

11. Holzworth, *Wild Grizzlies*, 154–55.

12. Ibid.

13. Coolidge to author, 19 November 1983.
14. Goodwin, interview with author, 29 March 1981.
15. AH to FHM, 17 May 1930, GFC.

Chapter 2: Minnesota Upbringing

1. Unless otherwise stated, the source of the quotations and other information in this chapter is FHM, "Not For All the Laurel Grows," Minnesota Historical Society, date unknown.
2. AH to FHM, 8 April 1943, GFC.
3. AH to A. Merritt, 26 April 1927, GFC.
4. Ibid.
5. AH to FHM, 22 August 1945, GFC.
6. Ibid.
7. Ibid., 28 October 1924, GFC.

Chapter 3: Outcast in Florida

1. Unless otherwise stated, the source of the quotations and other information in this chapter is FHM, "Not For All The Laurel Grows," Minnesota Historical Society, date unknown.
2. Coolidge to author, 4 August 1982.
3. AH to FHM, 5 July 1899, GFC. Many years later, when AH was in his late seventies, he told a newspaper reporter that he went up to Alaska with visions of striking it rich "in the gold fields" (Capt. Ernie Hall, "Sourdough Slides into Yacht Basin," AH Papers.)

Chapter 4: Northbound

1. AH to FHM, 26 May 1899, GFC.
2. Ibid., 13 June 1899.
3. Ibid., 5 July 1899.
4. Ibid., 14 November 1899.
5. In 1925, AH gave Coolidge this account of his departure for Alaska (from Coolidge to author, 4 August 1982). Many years later, he told newspaper reporters on two separate occasions that he had been the only member of the crew who had not

been shanghaied. (See also "Allen Hasselborg Says Bear Stories Don't Need Dressing," *Daily Alaska Empire*, 2 October 1950; and "Civilization Shy Alaskan Docks At Holmes Beach," AH Papers.)

6. Coolidge to author, 4 August 1982.

7. AH to FHM, 18 July 1900, GFC.

8. Ibid.

9. Ibid., 2 October 1900.

10. Ibid.

11. Ibid.

12. Ibid., 18 March 1901.

13. Ibid.

14. Ibid., 19 August 1901.

15. Ibid., 12 September 1901.

16. AH to Yaw, 21 May 1955, Sitka Pioneers' Home. The fort referred to here is Fort Chilkat.

17. FHM, "Not For All the Laurel Grows," Minnesota Historical Society.

18. AH to Yaw, 21 May 1955.

19. Lane, interview with author, 4 March 1981.

20. Young, *My Lost Wilderness*, 119; Lane, interview with author, 4 March 1981.

21. Lane, interview with author, 4 March, 1981.

22. Holzworth, *Wild Grizzlies*, 47–48; AH, from note in his copy of Holzworth, *Wild Grizzlies*, 329.

Chapter 5: The Best Woodsman

1. AH to MH, 3 January 1907, GFC; Stephens, "A Summer's Work," 268.

2. The 1907 Alexander Expedition to southeastern Alaska had at its disposal three shotguns, eight rifles, five pistols, seven thousand rounds of ammunition, and approximately four hundred leg-hold traps (Dixon to Grinnell, 6 April 1907, JG Papers).

3. Dixon to Grinnell, 2 May 1907, JG Papers.

4. Ibid.

5. Ibid.

6. Ibid., 2 June 1907.

7. Frederica de Laguna, an anthropologist and authority on Tlingit culture, provides the following explanation for the Tlingit name for Admiralty Island:

   "Our informants [Tlingit inhabitants of Admiralty Island c. 1950] referred to themselves as xutsnuwuwedi, 'People of the Brown Bear's Fort.' According to tradition, when the people first came to the site of Angoon. . . , a narrow strip of land between Kootznahoo Inlet on Admiralty Island and Chatham Strait, there were no trees on this peninsula and a bear or bears were seen walking around. So the people named the place xuts nuwu, 'Brown Bear's Fort.' The name is also applied to Admiralty Island as a whole, xutsnuwu x̱a't 'Brown Bear's Fort Island' . . . ." (de Laguna, *The Story of a Tlingit Community*, 25).

8. Stephens, "A Summer's Work," 569.

9. Dixon to Grinnell, 2 June 1907, JG Papers.

10. Ibid.

11. Ibid.

12. Ibid.

13. Ibid.

14. AH to MH, 16 June 1907, GFC.

15. AH, from note in his copy of Holzworth, *Wild Grizzlies*, 281–82.

16. Dixon to Grinnell, 4 July 1907, JG Papers.

17. Ibid., 20 August 1907.

18. Ibid.

19. Ibid.

20. AH to MH, 10 August 1907, GFC.

21. Ibid., 11 November 1907.

Chapter 6: Bitten by the Proud Bear

1. The University of California Museum of Vertebrate Zoology was inaugurated on March 23, 1908.

2. Alexander to AH, 8 February 1908, AH Papers.

3. Ibid., 25 November 1907.

4. Ibid., 10 March 1908.

5. Ibid., 8 February 1908.

6. Dixon to Grinnell, 9 February 1909, JG Papers.

7. Alexander to Grinnell, 10 March 1908, JG Papers.

8. Grinnell et al., "Birds and Mammals of the 1907 Alexander Expedition to Southeastern Alaska," 218.

9. AH to FHM, 15 February 1909, GFC.

10. Ibid.

11. AH, 1908 hunting journal, 1 April to 24 April 1908, AH Papers.

12. Ibid., 7 May.

13. Ibid., 1 June.

14. Ibid., 6 May.

15. Ibid., 27 September. Emmons recorded the Tlingit name for the glacier bear as "tskeek noon," or "gray blackbear" (Emmons, *The Tlingit Indians*, 133).

16. Ibid.

17. Alexander to AH, 1 June 1908, AH Papers.

18. A. Alexander was accompanied by Edmund Heller, a mammalogist who would join President Theodore Roosevelt's natural history expedition to Africa the following year, and Louise Kellogg, who would become Annie Alexander's lifelong companion.

19. Alexander's boat, the *Edna*, was built in sections in San Francisco, then shipped to Prince William Sound and assembled at Cordova.

20. Dixon to Grinnell, 6 August 1908, JG Papers.

21. AH, 1908 hunting journal, October 20, AH Papers.

22. AH to FHM, 15 February 1909, GFC.

23. Grinnell to AH, 19 March 1909, AH Papers.

24. AH to MH, 3 September 1909, GFC.

25. Alexander to Grinnell , 26 May 1909, JG Papers.

26. AH to FHM, 11 February 1911, GFC.

27. Merriam to AH, 16 May 1911 and 17 June 1911, AH Papers.

28. AH, 1911 hunting journal, August 4 and August 7–11, AH Papers.

29. AH to FHM, 22 November 1911, GFC.

30. Ibid., 20 July 1912.

31. Unless otherwise noted, this account of AH's encounter with a bear at Glacier Bay in 1912 is from Holzworth, *Wild Grizzlies*, 18–21; AH, notes in his copy of Holzworth, *Wild Grizzlies*, 18–21; R. Sheppard Jr. to author, 2 September 1984; *The Daily Alaska Dispatch*, 24 August 1912; and AH, notes in his copy of F. Hibben, "One Bite Is Enough" in *Hunting American Bears*, 176–98.

    F. Hibben's version of the incident, "One Bite Is Enough," was published by *True* magazine (September 1949) and as a chapter in *Hunting American Bears*. Hasselborg said Hibben's version was inaccurate. "That 'True' article was awfull," he told his family. "It got so much circulation that I got letters from all over the world which I wont answer. It was all fiction. Was with them, Mr. and Mrs. [Hibben], three trips taking bear pictures but they cant learn or write facts" (AH to FHM, 6 April 1950, GFC).

32. AH to FHM, 24 August 1912, GFC.

33. Dixon to AH, 12 December 1912, AH Papers.

34. Merriam to AH, 9 September 1912, AH Papers.

35. Ibid.

36. AH to RS, 24 September 1912, SFC.

37. Merriam, "Review of the Grizzlies and Big Brown Bears of North America" (1916), 69.

38. AH to Swarth, 26 November 1912, UCMVZ.

39. Young, *My Lost Wilderness*, 121.

40. AH to FHM, 6 March 1913, GFC.

41. AH to MH, 10 December 1913, GFC.

Chapter 7: Too Many Neighbors

1. AH to MH, 6 March 1913, GFC.

2. Gruening, *State of Alaska*, 143.

3. Ibid., 144.

4. AH to MH, 6 March 1913, GFC.

5. AH to FHM, 2 October 1900, GFC.

6. Impelled by his aversion to liquor, AH went to the polls in 1917 to help vote Alaska dry. In another uncharacteristic act of citizenship, he registered for the draft the following year.

7. AH to MH, 26 February 1914, GFC.

8. AH to Dixon, 1 April 1926, UCMVZ.

9. AH to FHM, 9 April 1924, GFC.

10. AH to FHM, 18 November 1918, GFC.

11. AH to I. Hasselborg, 3 May 1913, GFC.

12. Ibid.

13. AH to FHM, 7 November 1926, GFC; AH to MH, 28 March 1918, GFC.

14. AH to FHM, 12 March 1944, GFC.

15. Ibid.

16. V. L. Walker to AH, 15 December 1917, AH Papers.

17. AH to I. Hasselborg, 3 May 1913, GFC. One of the dam sites was at Hasselborg Lake. Hasselborg evidently had no qualms then about hydropower development on Admiralty Island. "There is 250 feet of fall from Hasselborg Lake and water enough and storage space enough to develop about 10 or 12,000 horse power," he told his brother Ira. "We located it for a big company and it will soon be used."

18. AH to MH, 10 December 1913, GFC.

19. Ibid.

20. Ibid., 26 February 1914.

21. AH to Swarth, 8 March 1916, UCMVZ.

22. AH always spelled *Bulldogg* with two "g's." That may have been his spelling of the word for a male chum (or "dog") salmon.

23. Merriam to AH, 28 March 1914, AH Papers.

24. AH to FHM, 18 January 1916, GFC. In 1915, Alaska's delegate to Congress sponsored a bill appropriating $750,000 to construct a bridge across Gastineau Channel. The first Juneau-Douglas bridge was not built until 1935, however.

25. de Laguna, *The Story of a Tlingit Community*, 32.

26. AH to MH, 8 February 1917, GFC; AH to J. Merritt, 16 April 1917, GFC.

27. AH to MH, 18 February 1917, GFC.

28. D. Stone and B. Stone, *Hard Rock Gold*, 21.

29. AH to MH, 14 May 1917, GFC.

30. Ibid.

31. AH to FHM, 2 July 1917, GFC.

32. AH to J. Merritt, 4 October 1917, GFC.

33. AH to FHM, 10 March 1946, GFC. AH's party on that excursion included a banker, M. H. Murch; a cameraman named Walker; and W. E. Bock, whom AH described as a "multimillionaire." In his letter to Flora, Hasselborg said that Walker shot "the first real movies of Alaska."

34. Rosenthal et al., *Admiralty... Island in Contention*, 23. AH also found two long-abandoned Tlingit village sites at Mole Harbor. Digging in his gardens, he would turn up many artifacts, including adzes, chisels, pestles, and whalebone harpoon heads. He donated most of them to the Alaska State Museum in Juneau. In 1949 he gave more than forty Tlingit artifacts to Frederica de Laguna, an anthropologist who stopped by to investigate the Mole Harbor sites. de Laguna noticed that AH had used fire-cracked rocks from the older of the two sites to build a long retaining wall near his cabin (de Laguna, *The Story of a Tlingit Community*, 32–33).

35. AH to FHM, 1 June 1918, GFC.

36. AH to MH, 28 March 1918, GFC.

37. Ibid., 5 September 1918.

38. AH to FHM, 18 November 1918, GFC; Holzworth, *Wild Grizzlies*, 43; AH, notes in his copy of Holzworth, *Wild Grizzlies*, 43.

39. AH to RS, 27 October 1924 and 1 July 1926, SFC.

40. Ibid., 27 October 1924.

41. Ibid., 3 November 1927.

42. AH to Swarth, 29 March 1918, UCMVZ.

43. Ibid.; AH to Swarth, 8 March 1918. Hasselborg's doubts about Dr. Merriam's classification of grizzly and brown bears were

apparently well-justified. In 1962, Ernest P. Walker, the ranking U.S. Biological Survey representative in Alaska during much of the period Merriam was studying bears, gave the following written statement to Dr. E. Raymond Hall, an authority on brown bear taxonomy:

"Ignore all specimens obtained by Merriam from fur dealers and persons who sold skulls to Merriam. Dr. Merriam sent word, for example, to Mr. X in Alaska that skulls were wanted from Admiralty Island. Mr. X told the Indians that bear skulls were wanted from Admiralty Island. The Indian hunters brought the skulls to Mr. X and told him that the skulls were from Admiralty Island. No wonder that four kinds of bears were recorded from Admiralty Island that had close relatives on the mainland. After skulls from Admiralty Island had been obtained, Dr. Merriam sent out word that skulls were wanted from the mainland. The fur dealers told the Indians and hunters, and the skulls that came in were all from the mainland, according to the hunters, regardless of where the bears were shot" (Hall to author, 10 June 1982).

Dr. Hall concluded: "It would seem that an accurate record of geographic variation to be found in skulls of grizzlies and big brown bears of southern Alaska might have to be made on the basis of skulls obtained before and after Dr. Merriam purchased skulls, or at least on skulls other than those purchased by Dr. Merriam" (ibid.).

44. See notes 37, 38, 39. According to his own estimate in 1926, AH shot "about 100 bears of different kinds" during his fourteen-year (1904–1918) career as a bear hunter (AH to RS, 1 July 1926, SFC). "Sportsmen that I have been out with have killed about 40 bears. The biggest I have killed had skins about 11 ft. across" (ibid.).

Chapter 8: Rancher

1. AH, 1927 weather journal, AH Papers.
2. AH to FHM, 1 June 1918, GFC.
3. Gruening, *State of Alaska,* 226.
4. AH to FHM, 1 April 1926, GFC. Some of the trees AH cleared for a garden near his cabin in 1916 were 90 to 100 years old (de Laguna, *The Story of a Tlingit Community,* 32).

5. Ibid., 9 April 1924.

6. Ibid., 9 September 1919.

7. Ibid.

8. AH to RS, 22 April 1923, SFC.

9. AH to FHM, 15 April 1925, GFC.

10. Ibid., 1 April 1926.

11. Ibid., 30 March 1928.

12. Ibid., 1 April 1926.

13. AH to RS, 22 April 1922, SFC.

14. AH to Dixon, 15 May 1929, UCMVZ.

15. AH to FHM, 30 March 1928, GFC.

16. AH weather journals, AH Papers: 27–29 September 1949; 5 September 1943; 30 November 1941; 19 January 1949; 2 August 1950.

17. AH had two gardens during his years at Mole Harbor. One was at the mouth of Mole River, about a quarter of a mile down from his cabin; the other was next to and behind his cabin. Other vegetables he mentioned planting were parsnips, spinach, celery, radishes, endives, kale, and brussel sprouts.

18. AH to FHM, 10 September 1941, GFC.

19. AH, weather journal, 19 June 1953, AH Papers.

20. AH to FHM, 4 September 1928, GFC.

21. The summer of 1917, not long after he moved out to Mole Harbor, AH had a small dog named Ginger to keep deer away from his garden. But he took her to town that fall, she wandered off, and someone shot her (AH to J. Merritt, 4 October 1917, GFC). He said later that if he ever got another dog (he never did) it would have to be small and not too fierce so the bears wouldn't kill it (AH to RS, 7 November 1926, SFC).

22. AH to Dixon, 7 July 1927, UCMVZ.

23. AH told one of his nephews that he usually carried a gun on his place in case a bear got "real bad" (AH to A. Merritt, 26 April 1927, GFC).

24. Lane, interview with author, 4 March 1981.

25. Young, *My Lost Wilderness*, 119.

26. AH to RS, 13 June 1922, SFC.

27. "There is an awfull fuss going on up here and in Wash[ington] trying to save the salmon, herring, ect.," AH wrote his brother, Horace, in 1925. "I am expecting to go on as a salmon stream guard right at my ranch. Havent found out yet if my politics (none) and religion (none) are all right. There will be 1000 or more guards this year and it will cost about a million. Mole Harbor where I live was a wonderfull fishing place but they fished the herring too hard and four years ago lost a purse seine with over 1000 bbls. herring and no herring or feeding salmon have come since" (AH to H. Hasselborg, 15 April 1925, GFC).

28. Lane, interview with author, 4 March 1981.

29. Ibid.

30. "I have got lots of young grouse and ducks and geese around my place just now, and as I dont bother them some are so tame they will walk right around me" (AH to RS, 1 July 1926, SFC); "The swallows came May 23 and raised 5 again. They have been out of the nest a week and will leave in a day or two" (AH to RS, 27 July 1934, SFC).

31. Frederica de Laguna, an anthropologist who did field research at Mole Harbor in 1949, remembered Hasselborg challenging her as soon as she set foot on the beach. Apparently he had heard that some anthropologists might be stopping by. "What are you, an anthropothagist?" he asked, testing her. de Laguna laughed, recognizing the scientific word for "cannibal," and they got on just fine after that (de Laguna, telephone conversation with author, 1983). See also Chapter 7, note 33.

32. AH to FHM, 19 October 1931, GFC.

33. Ibid.

34. AH to RS, 15 April 1930, SFC.

35. AH to FHM, 24 February 1931, GFC.

36. AH to A. Merritt, 15 March 1932, GFC.

37. Ibid.

38. "Have a deer about once a month in the fall," AH told his nephew Raymond Sheppard one year. "In the spring and summer eat trout mostly. There is so many trout in the pool in front of my house I can snag hook them without bait" (AH to RS, 27 October 1924, SFC). Occasionally he shot a Canada goose, but always regretted it: "About once in two years I get foolish and shoot at a flying goose with my little rifle and when I get him I

am mad enough to kick myself about having to pick him and cook him and then throw most of it out" (AH to RS, 26 April 1927, SFC).

39. AH to MH, 1 April 1926, GFC.

40. Holzworth, *Wild Grizzlies,* 12.

41. AH to FHM, 3 November 1927, GFC.

42. T. Davis, interview with author, 2 March 1981.

43. AH to FHM, 21 March 1933, GFC. AH was describing a visit from Mr. and Mrs. Stewart Edward White, the well-known writer of western novels, and his wife, who visited Hasselborg several times in the 1930s. Although Hasselborg demanded that his guests obey certain very strict rules, he was often a considerate host who showed his visitors the way up to the lakes or helped them catch trout in Mole River. A visitor from Boston, Teddy Holdsworth, remembered being taken out to watch humpback whales in Seymour Canal. Whenever the whales dived AH tried to predict where they were headed, then speeded over to wait for them to surface: "I was terrified," Holdsworth recalled "There we were in that sixteen-foot dory and those whales must have been sixty, seventy feet long" (T. Holdsworth, telephone conversation with author, 1983).

44. AH to FHM, 1930s, GFC.

45. Ibid.

46. AH weather journals: 1 March 1950; 20 February 1953; 29 June 1950; AH Papers

47. Hasselborg told Flora one fall that he had just canned seventy-six quarts of strawberries, currants, raspberries, and blueberries (AH to FHM, 12 September 1951, GFC).

48. AH weather journal, 28 November 1953, AH Papers.

49. AH to FHM, 28 October 1924, GFC. According to Stan Price, who knew Hasselborg in the period between the late 1930s and the early 1950s, Hasselborg loaded his own ammunition (Price, interview with author, 14 March 1981).

50. AH, 1953 weather journal, 7 November and 8 November, AH Papers.

51. AH to MH, 25 October 1925, GFC.

52. AH weather journal, 2 January 1953, AH Papers. The author found only a few precise accounts of Hasselborg's annual take

from his traps, most of which are in letters to his family and friends. It varied widely from year to year, depending on winter weather conditions and the game regulations. The winter of 1922, for example, he trapped 18 beaver, 11 weasels, 10 mink, and 6 marten. The following year, 22 beaver, 26 weasels, 16 mink, and 2 marten. Usually he sold his annual take for about $400. In 1937, he sold 14 marten, 12 mink, and 18 weasels for $600. One year in the late 1940s, fur prices were so high he made $1,500. Another year, he said the game regulations were so restrictive he made only $25.

53. AH to FHM, October 1937, GFC.

54. Ibid., 5 April 1938 and 4 October 1938.

55. In various letters to his family, Hasselborg mentioned reading Mark Twain's *Life on the Mississippi,* Voltaire's *Candide,* and *The Travels of Marco Polo.*

56. AH to FHM, 7 November 1926, GFC.

57. Ibid., 15 April 1925. James Oliver Curwood (1878–1927), a novelist and journalist, wrote adventure stories about Alaska and northern Canada that were quite popular among American readers in the 1920s and 1930s. Among his more than twenty-five books are *The Courage of Captain Plum* (1908); *The Grizzly King* (1916); *Nomads of the North* (1919); and *The Alaskan* (1923).

58. AH to FHM, 15 November 1944 and 13 September 1945, GFC.

59. Ibid., 7 November 1926.

60. AH to Swarth, 18 April 1919, UCMVZ.

61. Burg, "Fortress of the Bears," 26.

62. AH to FHM, 15 April 1925, GFC.

63. Goodwin, telephone conversation with author, 29 March 1981. During the 1920s, AH's cabin was robbed several times while he was in town. His solution, at least between 1925 and 1929, was to rig up guns set to shoot anyone who opened the cabin door or upstairs window. He then put word out that they were there (Holzworth, *Wild Grizzlies,* 134–36; AH notes in his copy of Holzworth, *Wild Grizzlies,* 134–36; Coolidge to author, 4 August 1982).

Harold J. Coolidge, who hunted with AH on Admiralty Island in 1925 (see Chapter 9), related the following incident: "On the day that we were leaving on his motor boat for me to return to Juneau, [AH] was working on his boat on the stream a little distance from his hut. I found that I had forgotten a piece of my equipment, and he had already locked up his shack. I started back to pick up the item that I left behind, and when he saw me doing so, he shouted for me to stop in a terrified, loud voice as if he had been physically injured. I returned to his boat to help him in his distress, and he told me that the reason he stopped me was that he had established a shotgun trap behind his door which could easily kill any intruder. (Coolidge to author, 4 August 1982).

64. Goodwin, telephone conversation with author, 29 March 1981.

65. AH to RS, 7 November 1926, SFC.

66. AH to MH, 19 April 1919, GFC.

67. AH to Swarth, 29 March 1918, UCMVZ.

68. Ebba Sheppard told FHM later that the toads hopped out of the box into her living room in Washington D.C. like young people eager to see the town (E. Sheppard to FHM, 1940s, GFC).

69. AH to MH, 8 March 1910, GFC.

70. AH to FHM, 2 July 1917, GFC.

71. Ibid., 18 November 1918.

72. AH to RS, 27 July 1934, SFC.

73. Ibid., 30 March 1935.

74. Ibid., 12 April 1936.

75. AH to FHM, 9 September 1919, GFC.

76. Ibid., 12 June 1920.

77. AH to RS, 13 June 1922, SFC.

78. AH to FHM, 8 November 1922, GFC. "There are two sea planes here now, makes me mad every time I see one," AH wrote in 1922. "And there are several hundred autos. Some day I am going to throw a stick of cordwood in the spokes of one when it tries to run me down" (AH to RS, 22 April 1922, SFC). That fall, when his nephew Raymond Sheppard reported that his parents had bought him a pony, Hasselborg said he was pleased by the news: "I think they are much nicer than a wicked old auto. I havent done anything to those autos yet as the police are neither of them friends of mine. Old Keegan is 6 ft. 6 in. and 300 lbs. and old Tibbets is about 5 ft. 3 and 100 lbs., but very vicious" (AH to RS, 12 October 1923, SFC).

79. AH to FHM, 6 June 1921, GFC.

80. AH to A. Merritt, 26 April 1927, GFC.

81. AH to Dixon, 13 March 1922, UCMVZ.

82. Ibid.; AH to MH, 7 November 1921, GFC.

83. AH, weather journals, 1 September 1947 and 19 April 1947, AH Papers.

Chapter 9: Bear Man

1. Unless otherwise stated, the quotations and most of the rest of the information in this account of AH's 1925 hunt with Harold J. Coolidge and Charles Day are from a letter H. Coolidge wrote to his father on 4 August 1925 (Coolidge family).

2. Coolidge described the canoe as "a light wooden one [Hasselborg] had built" (Coolidge, letter to his father, 4 August 1925, Coolidge family).

3. Coolidge to author, 4 August 1982.

4. Coolidge, letter to his father, 4 August 1925, Coolidge family.

5. Ibid.

6. D. Orth, *Dictionary of Alaska Place Names,* 154. Botany Peak was named by Hasselborg for the wide variety of wildflowers that grow there. Yellow Bear Mountain was named after the yellow bear shot by Coolidge and Day.

7. Burg, "Fortress of the Bears," 27.

8. T. Davis, interview with author, 2 March 1981.

9. By most accounts, the rifle Hasselborg carried while guiding photographers was a double-barrel Winchester .405. AH called it an "elephant gun" (T. Davis, interview with author, 2 March 1981). In 1927 he told Raymond Sheppard he had two .405s, a .45/70, a .30/30, and "a little model 53 Winchester .32/20 which I use for eagles and deer" (AH to RS, 3 November 1927, SFC). One of his notes in his copy of Holzworth, *Wild Grizzlies* (p. 75) indicates that he owned a .25/20 in the late 1920s. In the late 1930s he also had a .44/40 Winchester which now belongs to his great nephew, Raymond Sheppard, Jr.

10. Holzworth, *Wild Grizzlies,* 168–69.

11. Pack, "Bears of Admiralty," 80.

12. Ibid., 80–81.

13. Holzworth, *Wild Grizzlies,* 186–87. T. Davis also mentioned AH's practice of keeping two spare shells between the fingers of his left hand, ready for quick loading (Davis, interview with author, 2 March 1981).
14. Ibid., 53–54.
15. Dufresne, *No Room For Bears,* 138.
16. Ibid.
17. Ibid., 139.
18. Pack, "Bears of Admiralty," 130.
19. Ibid., 79.
20. T. Davis, interview with author, 2 March 1981.
21. F. Hibben, "Foolish Bears," in *Hunting American Bears*, 207–11.
22. Burg, "Fortress of the Bears," 27.
23. Holzworth, *Wild Grizzlies,* 62.
24. Ibid., 52.
25. AH note in his copy of Holzworth, *Wild Grizzlies,* 174.

Chapter 10: Wise in His Judgment

1. AH to FHM, 12 October 1923, GFC.
2. Goodwin, telephone conversation with author, 29 March 1981.
3. "Harold Coolidge wrote me last summer that he had told the President about my homestead and a lot of other things also, and sure enough I got the patent by the next mail" (AH to RS, 7 November 1926, SFC).
4. AH to FHM, 7 November 1926, GFC.
5. AH to Dixon, 7 July 1927, UCMVZ.
6. AH to RS, 7 November 1926, SFC.
7. AH notes in his copy of Holzworth, *Wild Grizzlies,* 4, 5, 38.
8. Ibid., 4, 38, 320.
9. AH note in his copy of Holzworth, *Wild Grizzlies,* xiv.
10. AH to FHM, 9 September 1928, GFC.
11. Ibid.
12. Ibid., 6 April 1934.
13. Ibid., 18 June 1929.

14. Ibid., 12 October 1929.

15. "Exterminate Brown Bears," *Daily Alaska Empire*, 21 October 1929.

16. "Protection of Brown Bear is to be Reduced," *Daily Alaska Empire*, 11 November 1929. Under the regulations that took effect 1 July 1930, bag limits and seasons remained in effect for hunters who were not Alaska residents and for Alaskans living in the northwestern part of the state (most significantly, on Kodiak Island). All Alaskans, however, could still legally kill a brown bear at any time in defense of life or property.

17. Sherwood, "Specious Speciation in the Political History of the Alaskan Brown Bear," 49.

18. Pack, "Bears of Admiralty," 80.

19. White, "The Truth About the Alaska Grizzly and Brown Bears," 278.

20. White, "Parking the Brown Bear," 38.

21. Holzworth, testimony before Special Committee on Conservation of Wild Life Resources, United States Senate, 18 January 1932.

22. "Plea is Made for Admiralty Bruin Preserve," *Daily Alaska Empire*, 22 March 1932.

23. C. Flory to B. F. Heintzleman, 1932, U.S. Forest Service archives, Juneau.

24. "Arguments for Bear Sanctuary Not Based on Fact," *Daily Alaska Empire*, 22 March 1932; "Regulations Give Assurance of Protection," *Daily Alaska Empire,* 18 June 1932.

25. Heintzleman, "Managing the Alaska Brown Bear," 332.

26. Ibid.

27. AH to FHM, 24 February 1931, GFC.

28. AH notes in his copy of Holzworth, *Wild Grizzlies,* 34, 12, 160.

29. AH to FHM, 24 February 1931, GFC.

30. AH note in his copy of Holzworth, *Wild Grizzlies,* title page: "by John Holzworth's authority, but written by Wm. Cumming, Prof. of English, Davidson College, N[orth] C[arolina] and somewhat rehashed by Mr. Holdsforth [sic]." In many other notes in his copy of *Wild Grizzlies* Hasselborg credits Cumming with writing the book. Trevor Davis, who chartered his boat, the

Cordelia D., to Hasselborg and Holzworth for their 1929 trip, confirmed Cumming's authorship (T. Davis, interview with author, 2 March 1981).

In other notes in his copy of *Wild Grizzlies,* AH credits many photographs in the book to Surratt, some of which are enlargements from movies Surratt took on his 1928 trip with Holzworth and Hasselborg.

31. AH notes in his copy of Holzworth, *Wild Grizzlies,* 73, 154.

32. Holzworth, *Wild Grizzlies,* 5.

33. AH note in his copy of Holzworth, *Wild Grizzlies,* 5.

34. T. Davis, interview with author, 2 March 1981; AH note in his copy of Holzworth, *Wild Grizzlies,* 37. AH made similar allegations in a letter to FHM (AH to FHM, 18 June 1929, GFC).

35. T. Holdsworth, telephone conversation with author, 1983.

36. AH note in his copy of Holzworth, *Wild Grizzlies,* 155.

37. AH note in his copy of Holzworth, *Twin Grizzlies,* 237; AH to FHM, 21 March 1933, GFC.

38. AH note in his copy of Holzworth, *Twin Grizzlies,* 250.

39. Ibid.

40. Ibid, 54.

41. Holzworth, *Twin Grizzlies,* 217–218, 87.

42. AH note in his copy of Holzworth, *Twin Grizzlies,* 217.

43. Ibid., 218.

44. Ibid.

45. Although Holzworth was apparently a persuasive lawyer and an effective political activist, he was by most accounts a strange, troubled man. Hasselborg's claim that Holzworth had been shell-shocked during World War I and had spent part of 1927 in a mental institution may well have been true. In 1932, he loudly disrupted the annual meeting of the National Audubon Society in Rochester, N.Y., "dancing up and down" and offering to fight anyone who tried to evict him (*New Rochelle Star,* 26 October 1932).

Alaska historian and longtime Juneau resident Robert DeArmond described Holzworth as "undoubtedly half a bubble, or more, off the beam" (DeArmond to author, 2 February 1982). Another Juneau resident, Karl Lane, said that

Holzworth was in and out of mental institutions most of his life (Lane, interview with author, 4 March 1981). Among AH's papers in the Gardner family collection is an undated, unidentified newspaper clipping which describes Holzworth's arrest for auto theft in Washington, D.C., his forced removal from a courtroom there, and a judge's decision to commit him to psychiatric care (GFC).

Holzworth was also a rather shady character, which lends credence to the rumor in Juneau that he was secretly working for pulp interests opposed to the development of the Alaska timber industry. In the early 1930s, at the height of the "Save-the-Bear Movement," a U.S. Forest Service official visiting New York discovered that the address on Holzworth's stationery was a Chinese laundry where he was told Holzworth occasionally picked up his mail (DeArmond to author, 2 February 1982). Other reports from that period variously describe him as the owner of a gun shop in New York City, a candidate for Congress, a friend of the president of the Alaska railroad, and an acquaintance of President Roosevelt. Trevor Davis alleged that Holzworth cheated several people, including Davis, out of hundreds of dollars during his trips to Alaska in the late 1920s and early 1930s (T. Davis, interview with author, 2 March 1981).

Victor Cahalane, a National Park Service official who met Holzworth several times, remembered hearing reports that he had absconded with money belonging to the New York Zoological Society (Cahalane to author, 31 August 1982).

46. Dixon, U.S. Park Service report, 1934.

47. "Arguments for Bear Sanctuary Not Based on Fact," *Daily Alaska Empire*, 22 March 1932.

48. By the 1920s, salmon runs had declined drastically in southeastern Alaska. Although the main cause was over-fishing, the government put some of the blame on brown bears and other animals that preyed on salmon. Bounties were offered on several species, including bald eagles. In 1924, Hasselborg admitted to Joe Dixon that he had been tempted by the one-dollar bounty for eagles. "I got the feet off of 110 eagles last year and at least 30 more felling dead trees back in the woods. Have just been reading an article in the 'Literary Digest' which made me try to blush with regard to this slaughter. I don't like this hunting business, but if I don't get them someone else would come along and shoot deer and other game besides. We have lots of game

laws but no enforcement" (AH to Dixon, 12 April 1924, UCMVZ).

49. "Arguments for Sanctuary Not Based on Fact," *Daily Alaska Empire*, 22 March 1932.

50. E. Sheppard to AH, 1932, AH Papers.

51. See note 6 above.

52. Frank Dufresne and J. P. Williams, Admiralty Island Bear Estimate; B. F. Heintzleman and H. W. Terhune. "A Plan for the Management of Brown Bear in Relation to Other Resources on Admiralty Island, Alaska," A clipping from *Stroller's Weekly* (no headline, undated) in the AH Papers quotes an estimate by AH of 800 to 1,000 bears on Admiralty Island. AH's notes on that clipping indicate that it was published in 1932, and that his actual estimate of the Admiralty Island bear population at that time was 600 to 1,000.

53. See notes 49, 52.

54. Young, *My Lost Wilderness,* 121.

Chapter 11: Hermit of Mole Creek

1. AH to FHM, 24 February 1931, GFC.

2. Ibid., 17 May 1930. AH told FHM in this letter that the "little girl" on the yacht "had her name, Dorothy Leadbetter, in letters of gold on her guns, her papa owns 4 or 5 pulp and paper mills and publishes the Portland 'Oregonian' and other papers."

3. Ibid.

4. Ibid.

5. Goodwin, telephone conversation with author, 29 March 1981.

6. AH to A. Merritt, 15 March 1932, GFC.

7. AH to FHM, 21 March 1933, GFC.

8. AH to FHM, 18 April 1939, GFC.

9. AH to RS, 6 April 1941, SFC.

10. AH to FHM, 18 April 1939, GFC.

11. Ibid., 20 June 1935.

12. Ibid., 20 September 1935.

13. Ibid., 6 April 1934.

14. Ibid., 8 April 1937.

15. Ibid., 20 September 1935.

16. In 1930, an aerial photograph of the interior of Admiralty Island was published in Holzworth's *Wild Grizzlies of Alaska* (p. 12). In his copy of *Wild Grizzlies,* AH labeled it a "navy plane picture." Dean Goodwin told the author that AH was upset that airplanes were taking away his guiding business (Goodwin, telephone conversation with author, 29 March 1981).

17. AH to FHM, 8 October 1940, GFC.

18. AH to RS, 6 April 1941, SFC.

19. AH to FHM, 4 October 1938, GFC.

20. Rakestraw, *History of the United States Forest Service in Alaska,* 116.

21. Ibid.

22. AH to FHM, 4 October 1938, GFC.

23. AH to RS, 6 April 1939, SFC.

24. AH to FHM, 18 April 1939, GFC.

25. Ibid., 17 March 1947. In 1931 Hasselborg got so fed up with the trapping laws he bought a small house on Douglas Island for "practically nothing," planning to stay there during the winter from then on. The former owner came back less than a year later, however, complaining about too many "bums" down south, and Hasselborg had to sell it back to him (AH to FHM, 24 February 1931 and 19 October 1931, GFC.).

26. AH to FHM, 5 April 1938, GFC.

27. Ibid.

28. Ibid.

29. Ibid., 11 August 1936.

30. Ibid., 20 June 1935.

31. Ibid., 15 September 1944.

32. AH to RS, 15 September 1937, SFC.

33. Ibid., 22 March 1942, SFC. During a nine-day inspection tour of Admiralty Island for the National Park Service in 1940, Victor Cahalane and Frank Bean, superintendent of Mount McKinley National Park, traveled from Mole Harbor to the north end of Hasselborg Lake and back. Before leaving Mole Harbor, they interviewed AH. "Allen Hasselborg's accusation that the bears had almost exterminated the beaver did not check with our

observations," Cahalane concluded (Cahalane, "Report of Inspection of Admiralty Island," 13).

34. Ibid.

35. F. Hibben, "Foolish Bears," in *Hunting American Bears,* 200.

36. F. Hibben, "Hasselborg's Hang-out," in *Hunting American Bears,* 153.

37. AH, 1938 weather journal, AH Papers: May 6, May 7, May 15, May 20.

38. This account of AH's encounter with a bear at Pleasant Bay in the late 1930s is from the author's interview with Stan Price on 14 March 1981. During the same interview, Price also described AH shooting a sow and her cub "sometime about '29, '30, along in there":

> Hasselborg shot a sow, and she had a cub, so he chained it up—drove a stick out there about 300 feet from his house, and the cub walked around that chain until he wore the grass down. After the fish were gone that fall, Al had nothing to feed him and it got bad, pestered him there, dug under his house, tore off the window shutters, knocked his woodpile down, and he had to shoot him. He didn't have any fish to feed him and if you haven't got fish to feed a bear, why, you're in trouble. Any place they can get their toenail in they take it apart. So he shot him and his hide was nailed on the side of the house there. Bill Woods and I and Jim Sawyer were there when he first had the cub out there. He was a friendly little cuss. That's a shame, you know, to tie up anything that's born in the wild. You can see it from the air. What the hell went around there? A merry-go-round? That's where Hasselborg had his cub tied to a stake.

39. "Allen Hasselborg, 79, Authority on Bears, Dies in Pioneers Home," *Juneau Empire,* 20 February, 1956; Alaska Geographic Society, Admiralty. . . Island in Contention, 23; Wooten, interview with author, 28 November 1991; T. Davis, interview with author, 2 March 1981. Davis told the author that AH said he had been mauled twice. Wooten told the author that the second mauling happened near Mole Harbor, and that AH had scars on his chest where the bear had raked him with its claws.

40. Olson, interview with author, 20 March 1981.

41. F. Hibben, "Hasselborg's Hang-out," in *Hunting American Bears,* 147–75. The version of AH's 1941 bear hunt with Frank Hibben given here incorporates comments and corrections AH made in

his copy of *Hunting American Bears,* and three letters to the author from Mrs. Frank C. Hibben (14 April 1982; 28 June 1982; 8 August 1982).

42. AH to FHM, 19 September 1942, GFC.

43. Ibid., 22 March 1942.

44. Young, *My Lost Wilderness,* 120.

45. Ibid.

46. Alaska Real Property Registration Law of March 24, 1945.

47. AH to FHM, 1 July 1946, GFC.

48. "'Not Factual' Says Noted Guide About Story on Himself," *Alaska Sunday Press,* 1 October 1950; "Allen Hasselborg Says Bear Stories Don't Need Dressing," *Daily Alaska Empire,* 2 October 1950.

49. O'Donnel, telephone conversation with author, 28 July 1981.

50. Ibid.

51. Olson, interview with the author, 20 March 1981.

52. Young, *My Lost Wilderness,* 114–16.

53. AH to FHM, 22 August 1945, GFC.

54. Lane, interview with author, 4 March 1981.

55. AH to FHM, 8 April 1951, GFC.

56. Ibid.

57. Ibid.

58. Ibid., 2 April 1945.

59. Undated clipping from unidentified newspaper, AH Papers.

60. AH to FHM, 28 September 1949, GFC.

61. Ibid., 6 April 1950.

62. Ibid., 8 April 1951.

63. Ibid., 2 September 1952.

64. Park, interview with author, April 1981.

65. Lane, interview with author, 4 March 1981.

66. Ibid.

67. "Leaving Bears and Homestead Behind, Hasselborg Pulls Up Admiralty Stakes," *Juneau Independent,* 17 September 1953; E. Sheppard to FHM, 13 August 1954, P. Sheppard Papers.

68. F. Wooten, telephone conversation with author, 28 November 1991.

69. "Leaving Bears and Homestead Behind, Hasselborg Pulls Up Admiralty Stakes," *Juneau Independent,* 17 September 1953.

70. Ibid.

71. "Civilization-Shy Alaskan Docks at Holmes Beach," AH Papers.

72. Park, interview with author, April 1981.

Chapter 12: Old Sourdough

1. E. Sheppard to FHM, 16 June 1954, GFC.

2. Ibid.

3. Ibid.

4. E. Gardner, interview with author, 10 June 1983.

5. Ibid.

6. E. Sheppard to FHM, 12 September 1954, GFC.

7. AH to FHM, 14 October 1954, GFC.

8. Capt. Ernie Hall, "Along the Waterfront," AH Papers.

9. "Civilization-Shy Alaska Docks At Holmes Beach," AH Papers.

10. E. Sheppard to FHM, 26 December 1954, GFC.

11. Ibid., 29 November 1954.

12. AH to FHM, 8 February 1955, GFC.

13. Ibid., 10 March 1955.

14. AH to Yaw, 21 May 1955, Sitka Pioneers' Home.

15. Ibid.

16. Keithahn to Yaw, 1955, Sitka Pioneers' Home.

17. AH to Yaw, 29 June 1955, Sitka Pioneers' Home.

18. AH to FHM, 25 July 1955, GFC.

19. AH to FHM, 8 November 1955, GFC; FHM, note written on letter from AH to FHM, 11 October 1955, GFC.

20. AH to FHM, 11 July 1955, GFC.

21. Park, interview with author, April 1981.

22. Yaw, telephone conversation with author, 1982.

23. Park, interview with author, April 1981.

Epilogue

1. Goodwin, telephone conversation with author, 29 March 1981.
2. Rakestraw, *History of the United States Forest Service in Alaska*, 114.
3. Price, interview with author, 14 March 1981.

BIBLIOGRAPHY

Archival Records

Alexander, Anne M. Correspondence and Papers, 1893–1939; 1904–1930; 1907–1949. Bancroft Library, University of California, Berkeley.

————. Field Notes, Prince William Sound, 1908. University of California Museum of Vertebrate Zoology, Berkeley, California.

Alaska Game Commission. Records, 1900–1920; 1906–1910. Smithsonian Institution, Archives Division, Washington, D.C.

Bayers, Lloyd H. ("Kinky"). Juneau Historical File, 1900–1954. Alaska Historical Library, Juneau.

Coolidge, Harold J. Letter to his father, August 4, 1925. Private Collection. Coolidge family.

Dixon, Joseph. Correspondence, 1907–1929. Historical Correspondence Files, University of California Museum of Vertebrate Zoology, Berkeley.

Grinnell, Joseph. Correspondence and Papers, 1884–1938; 1893–1939. Bancroft Library, University of California, Berkeley.

Hall, Ernie. "Sourdough Slides Into Yacht Basin," in "Along the Waterfront" column in unidentified Florida newspaper, 1954. Undated clipping in Allen Hasselborg Papers, Alaska Historical Library, Juneau, Alaska.

Hanscom, Bob. "Civilization-Shy Alaskan Guide Docks at Holmes Beach, Muses on Career," in unidentified Florida newspaper, 1954. Undated clipping in Allen Hasselborg Papers, Alaska Historical Library, Juneau, Alaska.

Hasselborg, Allen E. Letters, journals and miscellaneous documents. Alaska State Historical Library, Juneau, Alaska.

———. Letters to Raymond Sheppard, 1912–1953. Private Collection. Sheppard family.

———. Letters to Flora Hasselborg Merritt, 1899–1955. Private Collection. Gardner family.

———. Letters to Allen Merritt, 1920–1943. Private Collection. Gardner family.

———. Letters to J. Dixon, J. Grinnell, and H. Swarth: 1916–1929. Historical Correspondence files, University of California Museum of Vertebrate Zoology, Berkeley.

———. Field Notes, Southeast Alaska, 1908. University of California Museum of Vertebrate Zoology, Berkeley.

———. Field Notes, Prince William Sound, 1908. University of California Museum of Vertebrate Zoology, Berkeley.

———. Journal, Sitkan District, 1909. University of California Museum of Vertebrate Zoology, Berkeley.

———. Residents file, 1955. Sitka Pioneers' Home, Sitka, Alaska.

Heller, Edmund. Field-note books, Vol. 7, Prince William Sound Region, Alaska, 1908. University of California Museum of Vertebrate Zoology, Berkeley.

———. Papers and Photographs. Archives Division. Smithsonian Institution. Washington, D.C.

Merriam, C. Hart. California Journals: 1906–1918. Manuscript Division. Library of Congress. Washington, D.C.

———. Home journals, 1900–1918. Manuscripts Division. Library of Congress. Washington, D.C.

Merritt, Flora Hasselborg. Letters to Ebba Hasselborg Sheppard, 1954–1955. Private Collection. Sheppard family.

————. "Not for All the Laurel Grows." Minnesota Historical Society. St. Paul.

Pack, Arthur N., and William L. Finley (cinematographers). "The Great Bear of Alaska." Film (10 minutes, black and white, silent) produced by the American Nature Association, 1931. Film Archives of the Oregon Historical Society.

Powers, Richard L. "Public Involvement and Admiralty Island, Alaska." Master's thesis, University of Alaska Southeast, 1972.

Sheppard, Ebba Hasselborg. Letters to Flora Hasselborg Merritt, 1954–1955. Private Collection. Gardner family.

Stroller's Weekly, undated article (1932?) Allen Hasselborg Papers, Alaska Historical Library, Juneau, Alaska.

Swarth, H. Field Notes, Sitkan District, 1909. University of California Museum of Vertebrate Zoology, Berkeley.

————. Correspondence, 1912–1919, Historical Correspondence Files, University of California Museum of Vertebrate Zoology, Berkeley.

U.S. National Museum of Natural History. "Skins and Skulls" Catalogs, 1911–1925. Smithsonian Institution, Washington, D.C.

Walquist, Judith. "The History of Franconia." Franconia, Minnesota: Franconia Old Settlers Association, July 13, 1958.

Books and Articles

Alaska Geographic Society. *Admiralty . . . Island in Contention.* C. H. Rosenthal et al., editors. Anchorage: Alaska Geographic Society, 1973.

Alaska Sunday Press, 1 October 1950.

Burg, Amos. "Campfire Reflections." *Alaska Fish Tales and Game Trails* (November–December 1970).

————. "Fortress of the Bears." *Alaska Fish Tales and Game Trails* (Fall 1980).

Cahalane, Victor. *Report of Inspection of Admiralty Island, Alaska, 1942.* National Park Service. Washington, D.C., 1942.

Coolidge, Harold J. *Report on the Brown Bears of Admiralty Island.* U.S. Biological Survey, Washington, D.C., 1926.

Craighead, Frank C., Jr. *Track of the Grizzly.* San Francisco: Sierra Club Books, 1979.

Daily Alaska Dispatch. July 1, 1904; August 24, 1912; January–December 1913.

Daily Alaska Empire. October 21, 1929; November 11, 1929; January 30, 1932; March 3, 1932; March 22, 1932, June 6, 1932; June 18, 1932; August 9, 1932; October 2, 1950.

Davis, Trevor. *Looking Back on Juneau: The First Hundred Years.* Juneau: Miner Publishing Co., 1979.

De Armond, Robert N. "Juno's Days of Yore." *Info Juneau* (1985–1990).

de Laguna, Frederica. *The Story of a Tlingit Community.* Smithsonian Institution, Bureau of American Ethnology, Bulletin 172. Washington, D.C.: Government Printing Office, 1960.

Dixon, Joseph. U.S. Park Service report, 1934.

Dufresne, Frank. *No Room for Bears.* New York: Holt, Rinehart & Winston. New York: Random House, 1968.

Dufresne, Frank and J. P. Williams. *Admiralty Island Bear Estimate.* Tongass National Forest, Southeastern Alaska. USDA Forest Service and Alaska Game Commission. 12-page mimeo, 1932.

Emmons, George T. *The Tlingit Indians.* Edited with additions by Frederica de Laguna. American Museum of Natural History, Anthropological Paper No. 70. Seattle: University of Washington Press and the American Museum of Natural History, 1991.

Ferrell, Nancy. "Allen Hasselborg: Alaska Frontiersman." *Alaska* (June 1986).

Grinnell, Joseph. "Birds of the 1908 Alexander Alaska Expedition." *University of California Publications in Zoology* (March 1910).

Grinnell, Joseph, F. Stephens, J. Dixon, and E. Heller. "Birds and Mammals of the 1907 Alexander Expedition to Southeastern Alaska." *University of California Publications in Zoology* (1909).

Hall, E. R. *North American Mammals*. New York: Random House, 1981.

Heintzleman, B. F. "Managing the Alaska Brown Bear." *American Forests* (June 1932).

Heintzleman, B. F., and H. W. Terhune. "A Plan for the Management of Brown Bear in Relation to Other Resources on Admiralty Island, Alaska." U.S.D.A. Misc. Pub. No. 195. Washington, D.C., 1934.

Heller, Edmund. "Mammals of the 1908 Alexander Alaska Expedition." University of California Publications in Zoology (March 1910).

Hibben, Eleanor. "It's a Man's World." *Forest and Stream* (November 1949).

Hibben, Frank C. "Foolish Bears." *Forest and Stream (November 1946)*.

————. *Hunting American Bears*. Albuquerque: University of New Mexico Press, 1945.

————. "One Bite is Enough." *True* (September 1949).

Holzworth, John M. *The Wild Grizzlies of Alaska*. New York and London: G. P. Putnam's Sons, 1930.

————. "Sanctuary for Alaskan Bears." *Outdoor Life* (January 1932).

————. *The Twin Grizzlies of Admiralty Island*. Philadelphia and London: J. P. Lippincott Co., 1932.

Jonaitis, Aldona. *Art of the Northern Tlingit*. Seattle and London: University of Washington Press, 1986.

Juneau Empire. February 20, 1956.

Juneau Independent. September 17, 1953.

Kamenskii, Fr. Anatolii. *Tlingit Indians of Alaska*. Translated by Sergei Kan. The Rasmuson Library Historical Translations Series, Vol. 2. Fairbanks: University of Alaska Press, 1985.

Lawrence, A., W. S. Webb, and A. B. Hallowell. "Summer on Admiralty Island." *Sportsman* (February 1932).

Merriam, C. Hart. "Descriptions of Thirty Apparently New Grizzly and Brown Bears of North America." *Proceedings of the Biological Society of Washington* (August 13, 1914).

———. "Nineteen Apparently New Grizzly and Brown Bears from Western America." *Proceedings of the Biological Society of Washington* (September 1916).

Merriam, C. Hart. "Review of the Grizzlies and Big Brown Bears of North America." U.S. Department of Agriculture, Bureau of Biological Survey North American Fauna, No. 41. Washington, D.C., 1918.

New Rochelle Star, 26 October 1932.

Orth, Donald J. *Dictionary of Alaska Place Names.* Geological Survey Professional Paper 567, U.S. Department of the Interior. Washington, D.C.: Government Printing Office, 1967.

Pack, Arthur N. "Bears of Admiralty." *Nature* (February 1932).

Rakestraw, Lawrence. "A History of the United States Forest Service in Alaska." Alaska Department of Education, Historical Commission. Anchorage, Alaska, 1981.

Riggs, Thomas, Jr. Annual Report of the Governor of Alaska to the Secretary of the Interior, 1919. Washington, D.C.: U.S. Department of the Interior, 1920.

Roderick, Barry. *A Preliminary History of Admiralty Island: 1794–1942.* Juneau, Alaska: U.S. Department of Agriculture, Forest Service, 1982.

Roppel, Patricia. *Southeast Alaska: A Pictorial History.* Norfolk, Virginia: Donning Company, 1983.

Russell, Andy. *Grizzly Country.* New York: Alfred A. Knopf, 1968.

Schoen, John. W., Sterling D. Miller, and Harry V. Reynolds III. "Last Stronghold of the Grizzly." *Natural History* (January 1987).

Shepard, Paul and B. Sanders. *The Sacred Paw.* New York: Viking Penguin, 1985.

Sherwood, Morgan. *The Exploration of Alaska.* New Haven: Yale University Press, 1965; reprint, with a preface by Terrence Cole, Fairbanks: University of Alaska Press, 1992.

————. "Specious Speciation in the Political History of the Alaskan Brown Bear." *Western Historical Quarterly* (January 1979).

————. *Big Game in Alaska: A History of Wildlife and People.* New Haven: Yale University Press, 1981.

Simpson, Sherry. *Juneau.* Anchorage: Alaska Geographic Society, 1990.

Smith, D. C. "Pulp, Paper and Alaska." *Pacific Northwest Quarterly* (April 1975).

Sorensen, Conner. "Historic Resources of Admiralty Island National Monument, Alaska." Juneau: Self–published, 1980.

Stephens, Frank. "A Summer's Work: A Natural History Expedition to Southeastern Alaska." *Forest and Stream* (October 10, 1908).

Sterling, Keir B. *Last of the Naturalists: The Career of C. Hart Merriam.* New York: Arno Press, 1974

Stone, David, and Brenda Stone. *Hard Rock Gold.* Juneau, Alaska: Juneau Centennial Committee, City and Borough of Juneau, 1980.

Thornton, Thomas F. "Subsistence Use of Brown Bear in Southeast Alaska." Technical paper No. 214. Juneau: Alaska Department of Fish and Game, Division of Subsistence, 1992.

Turner, Frederick Jackson. "The Significance of the Frontier in American History." Address delivered at a meeting of the American Historical Association in Chicago, 12 July 1893. In *The Early Writings of Frederick Jackson Turner.* Madison: University of Wisconsin Press, 1938, 185–229.

U.S. Senate. *Brown Bear of Alaska: Hearing before the Special Committee on Conservation of Wild Life Resources.* 72d Congress, 1st session, January 18, 1932.

White, Stewart Edward. "Parking the Brown Bear." *Saturday Evening Post* (March 7, 1931).

————. "Alaska's Brown Bears." *American Forests* (May 1932).

————. "The Truth About the Alaska Grizzly and Brown Bears." *American Forests* (May 1932).

237

———. "Our Great Bears." *Field and Stream* (February 1935).

Young, Ralph W. *Grizzlies Don't Come Easy*. Tulsa, Oklahoma: Winchester Press, 1981.

———. *My Lost Wilderness*. Tulsa, Oklahoma: Winchester Press, 1983.

Interviews

Beier, LaVern (biologist, Alaska Department of Fish and Game)

Coolidge, Harold J. (zoologist, Massachusetts)

Davis, Trevor and Carol Davis (acquainted with A. Hasselborg)

De Armond, Robert N. (historian, Juneau)

de Laguna, Frederica (anthropologist)

Gardner, Elinor (Hasselborg family)

Goodwin, Dean (acquainted with A. Hasselborg)

Hibben, Frank C. (acquainted with A. Hasselborg)

Holdsworth, Teddy (acquainted with A. Hasselborg)

Lane, Karl (acquainted with A. Hasselborg)

McNight, Don (part-owner of Hasselborg homestead)

Moss, Madonna (anthropologist, U.S. Forest Service)

O'Donnell, Jack (acquainted with A. Hasselborg)

Olson, Sigurd (acquainted with A. Hasselborg)

Park, Tom (acquainted with A. Hasselborg)

Price, Stan (acquainted with A. Hasselborg)

Schroeder, Elaine (psychologist, Juneau)

Wallen, Richard T. (biologist, Juneau)

Wooten, Jerry (acquainted with A. Hasselborg)

Yaw, Leslie (Sitka Pioneers' Home)

Correspondence

Cahalane, Victor H. (National Park Service, retired)

Coolidge, Harold J. (zoologist, Massachusetts)

De Armond, Robert N. (historian, Juneau)

de Laguna, Frederica (anthropologist, Bryn Mawr College)

Gardner, Elinor (Hasselborg family)

Hall, E. Raymond (University of Kansas)

Hibben, Mrs. Frank C. (acquainted with A. Hasselborg)

Leer, Jeff (Alaska Native Language Center)

Moss, Madonna (U.S. Forest Service)

Sheppard, Raymond, Jr. (Hasselborg family)

Young, Ralph (acquainted with A. Hasselborg)

INDEX

JOHN R. HOWE currently resides in Cambridge, Massachusetts, where he directs an Internet/World Wide Web site for writers and publishers. Between 1980 and 1992, while writing this book, he lived in Juneau, Alaska, working as a videographer, freelance writer, teacher, and conservationist. His articles on wildlife subjects have been published in *Audubon, Defenders,* and *Alaska* magazines. He is a graduate of Stanford University and holds a masters degree in sociobiology and communications from San Francisco State University.

LanternLight
LIBRARY

Bear Man of Admiralty Island is the second volume in the LanternLight Library series of informal nonfiction about the north—readable and informative, worth putting into a backpack before setting off across tundra or through rainforest. If you have room for only one book, it should be a LanternLight—just right for reading in the warm glow of a camp lantern, far from the nearest library.